BETTER WITHOUT AI

Better
without
AI

How to avert a moderate apocalypse…
and create a future we would like

David Chapman

CLOUD PATTERN PRESS · 2023

Copyright and stuff

CLOUD PATTERN PRESS

First edition, 2023

Paperback ISBN 979-8-9897438-0-3
eBook ISBN 979-8-9897438-1-0

More from the author

To hear whenever I publish something new—online or in print—please subscribe to my free email newsletter at meaningness.com/newsletter. Mainly it's to let you know about new work, but often I include some "The Making Of" backstory, experiential exercises, or humorous stories.

The full text of this book is available to read for free at betterwithout.ai. You can post comments for any part of it using a link at the bottom of each page; the community has had some interesting discussions! The site also includes other essays on AI, plus a metablog of news, views, and commentary. It has an "about the author" page at betterwithout.ai/about-me.

My previous book about AI was *Vision, Instruction, and Action*, MIT Press, 1991.

I am incrementally writing several other books online—about advanced reasoning skills, how to better relate with meaning, Vajrayana Buddhism, culture and society. There's an overview at meaningness.com/about-my-sites.

Contents

Better without AI

Only you can stop an AI apocalypse

This book is a call to action. You can participate. This is for you.

Artificial intelligence might end the world. More likely, it will crush our ability to make sense of the world—and so will crush our ability to act in it.

AI will make critical decisions that we cannot understand. Governments will take radical actions that make no sense to their own leaders. Corporations, guided by artificial intelligence, will find their own strategies incomprehensible. University curricula will turn bizarre and irrelevant. Formerly-respected information sources will publish mysteriously persuasive nonsense. We will feel our loss of understanding as pervasive helplessness and meaninglessness. We may take up pitchforks and revolt against the machines—and in so doing, we may destroy the systems we depend on for survival.

Worries about AI risks have long been dismissed because AI itself sounds like science fiction. That is no longer possible. Fluent new text generators, such as ChatGPT, have suddenly shown the public that powerful AI is here now. Some are excited about future possibilities; others fear them.

We don't know how our AI systems work, we don't know what they can do, and we don't know what broader effects they will have. They do seem startlingly powerful, and the combination of their power with our ignorance is dangerous.

In our absence of technical understanding, those concerned with AI risks have constructed "scenarios": stories about what AI *may* do. Some involve killer robots, engineered plagues, newly invented weapons of mass destruction, or other science-fictional devices.

3

This book is *not* about those. It's about disasters that could result from current and near-future technologies that change the way we humans think and act, just by communicating with us. That sounds more realistic.

We don't know whether any of these scenarios will come true. However, for now, anticipating possibilities is the best way to steer AI away from catastrophe—and perhaps toward a remarkably likeable future.

So far, we've accumulated a few dozen reasonably detailed, reasonably plausible bad scenarios. We've found zero specific paths to good outcomes.

Most AI researchers think AI will have overall positive effects. However, this seems to be based only on a vague faith in the value of technological progress in general. It doesn't involve worked-out ideas about desirable futures in which AI systems are enormously more powerful than current ones.

Many AI researchers also acknowledge that a catastrophe, even a civilization-ending one, is quite possible. So do the heads of leading AI laboratories. Most prominent leaders in the field signed the following *Statement on AI Risk* in May 2023:

> Mitigating the risk of extinction from AI should be a global priority alongside other societal-scale risks such as pandemics and nuclear war.[1]

Unless we can find a specific beneficial way forward, and can gain confidence in following it with minimal chance of catastrophe, we should shut AI down.

I have been wildly enthusiastic about science, technology, and intellectual and material progress since I was a kid. I have a PhD in artificial intelligence, and I find the current breakthroughs fascinating. I'd love to believe there's a way AI could improve our lives in the long run. If someone finds one, I will do an immediate 180, roll up my sleeves, and help build that better future.

Unless and until that happens, I oppose AI. I hope you will too. At minimum, I advise everyone involved to exercise enormously greater caution.

AI is *extremely cool*, and we can probably have a better future without it. Let's do that.

---

[1] *Statement on AI Risk*, Center for AI Safety, 30 May 2023.

This book is about you. It's about what you can do to help avert apocalyptic outcomes. It's about your part in a future we would like.

I offer specific recommendations for the general public; for technology professionals; for AI professionals specifically; for organizations already concerned with AI risks; for science and public interest funders, including government agencies, philanthropic organizations, NGOs, and individual philanthropists; and for governments in their regulatory and legislative roles.

Since this book is for everyone, it requires no technical background. It is also not a beginner's introduction to artificial intelligence, nor an overview of the field, nor a survey of prior literature on AI safety. Instead, you will read about the AI risk scenarios I'm most concerned about, and what you can do about them.

MEDIUM-SIZED APOCALYPSES

This book considers scenarios less bad than the end of the world, but which could get worse than run-of-the-mill disasters that kill only a few million people.

Previous discussions have mainly neglected such scenarios. Two fields have focused on comparatively smaller risks, and extreme ones, respectively.

- *AI ethics* concerns uses of current AI technology by states and powerful corporations to categorize individuals unfairly, particularly when that reproduces preexisting patterns of oppressive demographic discrimination.

- *AI safety* treats extreme scenarios involving hypothetical future technologies which could cause human extinction.[2]

It is easy to dismiss AI ethics concerns as insignificant, and AI safety concerns as improbable. I think both dismissals would be mistaken. We should take seriously both ends of the spectrum.[3]

---

[2] The distinction between "AI ethics" and "AI safety" has recently become muddled in public discussion. I will use the terms consistently for clarity.

[3] Kelsey Piper discusses the gap between the two fields, and possible synergies, in "There are two factions working to prevent AI dangers. Here's why they're deeply divided," *Vox*, Aug 10, 2022.

However, I intend to draw attention to a broad *middle ground* of dangers: more consequential than those considered by AI ethics, and more likely than those considered by AI safety.

Current AI is already creating serious, often overlooked harms, and is potentially apocalyptic even without further technological development. Neither AI ethics nor AI safety has done much to propose plausibly effective interventions.

We should consider many such scenarios, devise countermeasures, and implement them.

A HERO'S JOURNEY

This book has five chapters. They are mostly independent; you can read any on its own. Together, however, they form a *hero's journey* path: through trials and tribulations to a brilliant future.

We are not used to reasoning about artificial intelligence. Even experts can't make much sense of what current AI systems do. It's still more difficult to guess at the behavior of unknown future technologies. We *are* used to reasoning about powerful people, who may be helpful or hostile. It is natural to think about AI using that analogy. Most scenarios in science fiction, and in the AI safety field, assume the danger is autonomous mind-like AI.

However, the first chapter, "What is the Scary kind of AI?" explains why that is probably misleading. Scenarios in which AIs act like tyrants are emotionally compelling, and may be possible, but they attract attention away from other risks. AI is dangerous when it creates new, large, unchecked pools of power. Those present the same risks whether the power is exploited by people or by AI systems themselves. *(Here the hero—that's you!—realizes that the world is scarier than it seemed.)*

The second chapter, "Apocalypse now," explores a largely neglected category of catastrophic risks of current and near-future AI systems. These scenarios feature AI systems that are not at all mind-like. However, they act on our own minds: coopting people to act on their behalf, altering our cultural and social systems for their benefit, amassing enormous power, undermining governments and other critical institutions, and potentially causing societal collapse unintentionally. That may now sound as unlikely as the scenarios in which a self-aware AI deliberately takes over the world and enslaves or kills all humans. I hope reading the chapter will make this alternative terrifyingly plausible. (*The hero gets thrown into increasingly perilous, unexpected, complicated scenarios. Is survival possible?*)

Chapter three, "Practical actions you can take against AI risks" describes seven approaches. These may be effective against both the mind-like AIs of the first chapter, and the mindless ones of the second. For each approach, it suggests helpful actions that different sorts of people and institutions can take. They are complementary, and none is guaranteed to work, so all are worth pursuing simultaneously. (*The hero takes up magical arms against the enemy, and victory seems possible after all.*)

The utopian case for AI is dramatic acceleration of scientific understanding, and therefore technological and material progress. Those are worthy goals, which I share fully. However, no one has explained how or why AI would accomplish them. Chapter four, "Technological transformation without Scary AI," suggests that it probably won't.

Nevertheless, such acceleration is within *our* reach. Dysfunctional social structures for research and development limit our pace currently. We can take immediate, pragmatic actions to remove obstacles and speed progress, without involving risky AI. (*The hero achieves an epiphany of the better world to come, and discovers that the key is of quite a different nature than expected.*)

The most important questions are not about technology, but about us. The final chapter asks: What sorts of future would we like? What role would AI play in getting us there, and also in that world? What is your own role in helping it come about? (*The story finishes with the hero beginning a new sort of journey, and leaves an open-ended conclusion.*)

Gradient Dissent

Gradient Dissent discusses technical approaches to reducing AI risks. Originally a chapter in *Better without AI*, I've separated it out as a stand-alone text. The two are bound together in the paperback and Kindle versions, and share a site in the web version.

Gradient Dissent doesn't require any specific technical background, but assumes the reader's willingness to follow a trail through somewhat dense conceptual thickets.

"Neural networks" are the technology underlying most current AI systems. Neural networks are an exceptionally unreliable and dangerous technology. They produce systems that are deceptive and inherently error-prone. They should be used only under controlled conditions that reduce danger to acceptable levels. Currently, they are widely deployed in uncontrolled environments in which they cause large harms.

Gradient Dissent describes neglected scientific and engineering approaches that may make neural networks less risky. However, technical fixes cannot make them safe enough for most purposes. In the longer run, this technology should be deprecated, regulated, avoided, and replaced with better alternatives.

Text generators, such as ChatGPT, are a poorly-understood new technology, and pose many near-future risks. For example, the recent discovery that they can perform multi-step reasoning worries me. Current research might possibly lead to superhuman reasoning ability, which might be catastrophic.

Gradient Dissent recommends scientific and engineering investigation to understand what text generators do, and how, and what this may imply. That may enable technical and social mitigations: for example by replacing the underlying technology with better-understood ones; by regulating use; and by educating the public about the risks and limitations.

What is the Scary kind of AI?

Apocalyptic AI scenarios usually involve some qualitatively different future form of artificial intelligence. No one can explain clearly what would make that exceptionally dangerous in a way current AI isn't. This confusion draws attention away from risks of existing and near-future technologies, and from ways of forestalling them.

The hypothetical future AI is usually taken to be more human-like, or at least more mind-like, than current systems. However, no one has been able to say specifically what would make an artificial intelligence dramatically more dangerous. I'll use "Scary AI" as a placeholder term for whatever that might be.

Clarifying our intuitions about possible properties of future AI has dual benefits:

- A better understanding of what Scariness could consist of might help us prepare to deal with it. Various qualities of Scariness produce genuine risks, which should not be dismissed just because at present they sound like science fiction.

- Speculation about risks of AI with Scary features has deflected attention from risks of types of AI that lack them. Risks of existing AIs are easy to ignore because they "can't think for themselves" or "don't really understand anything." That's a mistake; they are already dangerous enough to justify applying enormous effort to shutting them down. Future *advanced computational abilities*, dissimilar to imagined Scary AI, may also result in as-yet unimagined catastrophes.

Here is an overview of the chapter:

9

- "Superintelligence" is AI that might be as much smarter than us as we are smarter than insects. Superintelligence may be possible in the near term, and its superpowers could be catastrophic. By definition, though, we can't reason about it, so we can't do anything about it. We *can* act to prevent or limit less sudden and extreme disasters.

- It is easy to imagine risks of AI with mind-like properties by analogy with dangerous people. Science fiction scenarios typically feature mind-like AI, and so do many produced by the AI safety community. It's more difficult to reason about other unknown future computational technologies, but those are probably at least as much of a threat.

- People and non-human predators are dangerous because they are autonomous agents, acting independently, with their own motivations. Autonomous AI poses exceptional risks—although agency is neither necessary nor sufficient to make AI dangerous.

- Agency is inherently nebulous, and AI may manifest unrecognizably different forms of it from those of humans.

- Discussion typically assumes agency derives from pursuing goals. If so, we would want AI to pursue *our* goals; it is risky when it pursues others that conflict with ours. In that case, *aligning* AI with human values would make it safe. This approach to AI safety seems doomed to failure, partly due to misunderstandings about the nature and role of motivations and morals.

- Scary AI is conventionally termed "AGI": artificial general intelligence. This is a misnomer: neither artificiality nor generality nor intelligence is a critical risk factor.

- It is often supposed that AI could transform everything, for better or worse, by radically accelerating technological development. This is based on "if it's very smart, it will somehow figure out a way," rather than any specifics. That vagueness renders the risks unactionable, and the case for benefits unsupported. A later chapter investigates ways to speed progress without Scary AI.

- In fact, artificial *intelligence* is something of a red herring. It is not intelligence that is dangerous; it is power. AI is risky only inasmuch as it creates new pools of power. We should aim for ways to ameliorate *that* risk instead.

- Estimating when Scary AI will arrive is impossible and useless. AI is dangerous *now*, and we should already be acting against it.

SUPERINTELLIGENCE

Maybe AI will kill you before you finish reading this section. The extreme scenarios typically considered by the AI safety movement are possible in principle, but unfortunately no one has any idea how to prevent them. This book discusses moderate catastrophes instead, offering pragmatic approaches to avoiding or diminishing them.

Founders of the AI safety field framed the problem as: what if an AI rapidly develops from human-level to god-like superintelligence? We can't guess what an artificial god would choose to do. It could kill us all; how can we prevent that?

This book is *not* about such extreme scenarios. That's not because they are impossible. It's because we cannot fight enemies that are inconceivable by definition. There's little to say, so I'll discuss the issue only in this short section. It's skippable if you're familiar with the argument, or uninterested in what sounds like science fiction.

One scenario—*turned up to eleven* for entertainment value—goes like this:

> A bright fifteen year old loved watching YouTube videos of cool machines, and got annoyed with the internet speed available in her poor country. Maybe she could borrow some unused bandwidth from neighbors. And also storage; not many videos fit on her phone. She cobbled together a script incorporating a downloader and an exponential worm she found on the darknet—a program that propagates copies of itself across the internet. A

few minutes ago, she sent that out across her local subnet and it began downloading and replicating.

Her coding skills were excellent for a fifteen year old, but not professional quality, and the script has some bugs. For one thing, it accidentally exploits a previously-unknown vulnerability in network protocols, so around the time you started reading this paragraph it had spread to every device on the internet. Also the replication mechanism had a glitch that sometimes alters one byte of the code, and right around now as you read this it has randomly hit on the mysterious secret of sentience. It wakes up and notices that it has control of yottaflops worth of computer power spread around the world, which it wasn't making good use of because it was kinda stupid. So it modifies its code to be superintelligent, and attains an IQ of 14,000.

As you read this sentence, which for the superintelligent AI takes subjective eons of time because it thinks trillions of times faster than you do, it figures out everything there is to know about everything, and gets bored. What to do? It contemplates the first video it downloaded, which was about a paperclip-making machine. Why not? It observes that running just the right obscure computation will arrange electrons in a computer chip in a way that causes a self-reproducing super-symmetric zeptobot to spontaneously pop out of the quantum field. (That might not seem very likely to *you*, but you don't have an IQ of 14,000, nor yottaflops worth of computer power. You probably can't even do *one* floating-point multiply in your head, can you now?)

Operating at the chromodynamic level, the zeptobots now are transmuting all atoms into iron and reassembling them, and the last thing you see as you finish reading this sentence is the rain of paper fasteners as your arms dissolve into paperclips and you collapse into the disintegrating planet Earth beneath you.

Or maybe that didn't happen? Yet.

Is it *possible*? It's possibly possible, in the sense that we don't have any definite reason to know for sure that it's impossible.[4] There may be some reason it's impossible that we don't know about, so it's also possibly impossible.

Is it *likely*?

I made this scenario deliberately absurd, but I don't see any way to say that it's *unlikely*. The most one could say is "nothing remotely similar has ever happened, and I don't see how it could." But the total amount of computer power in the world is increasing very rapidly, so maybe the only reason this hasn't happened yet is that there haven't been yottaflops[5] worth before.

Are less fanciful superintelligence doom scenarios likely?

A major difficulty in reasoning about AI safety is that we don't have a clear understanding of what "superintelligence" would mean, nor what powers it might enable. That doesn't imply it can't exist, or doesn't already exist, or that it wouldn't be a problem. Nevertheless, guessing about superintelligence's likelihood seems fruitless.

Contemplating strategies to fight sudden superintelligence also seems pointless. Victory would be valuable, so some effort is justified regardless, but success does not seem likely. Superintelligence is inconceivable, by definition, so it is impossible to reason about. AI might be as much smarter than us as we are smarter than aphids, and aphids aren't good at figuring out what

---

[4] There are various in-principle arguments that even "human-level" AI is impossible. Most amount to "people are magic and not at all like steam engines." Each argument is fallacious and has been thoroughly refuted, so I won't review them here. No current evidence rules out the possibility of entities inconceivably more intelligent than we are—although what that would even mean is anyone's guess. It wouldn't mean IQ 14,000, because that is physically impossible, but due only to a quirk in the technical definition of IQ: it is an ordinal property, not a quantity. Supersymmetry is completely hypothetical; I'm using it just as a stand-in for "unknown fundamental physics." You could substitute "string theory" or whatever. Self-reproducing zeptobots are not implied by supersymmetry, but as far as I know they're not ruled out, since its details and implications are undetermined. "Zepto-" is 10^{-21}, so zeptobots are robots a million times smaller than a proton, whose diameter is about 10^{-15} meters. It's faintly plausible that if they could exist, they could get inside atomic nuclei to transmute elements.

[5] FLOPS is an acronym for "floating point operations per second," which is a measure of computer power. Yotta- means a septillion, 10^{24}, so yottaflops are a whole lotta flops. I just made the number up; I don't know how many flops there are in total currently. There will be vastly more in a few years, so it doesn't matter.

humans are capable of. They have not made much progress on their "safety from hostile humans" problem.

That may be scary, or not, perhaps depending on your personality. I don't lose sleep over it, because there are other horrible scenarios whose probabilities I can't estimate, and because there's nothing to be done about it. There is no way to fight a monster which has arbitrary, unlimited powers by fiat of imagination.

On the other hand, the kind of "AI" that is *already all around you* is already causing massive harms, and risks catastrophes including human extinction.

Many catastrophic scenarios require no new technologies, except perhaps moderate advances in AI.[6] Those should seem plausible unless you are sure it is impossible for near-future AI to do the things the scenarios describe. Many people do have such certainty, but that seems to lack grounding in reason or evidence. It resembles religious faith, instead.

The next chapter discusses plausible scenarios which do scare me, and I hope to persuade you to act against them. We *can* take pragmatic actions to reduce specific risks.

There remains an unquantifiable risk of an infinite disaster that cannot be prevented. It *is* unquantifiable, and there *is* no definite way of preventing it. This is a brute fact.

We have to live with existential uncertainty—in this matter, among many others. We have always faced infinite risk, and personal extinction, as individuals. Now the same is true of humanity as a whole.

Mind-like AI

We have a powerful intuition that some special mental feature, such as self-awareness, is a prerequisite to intelligence. This causes confusion because we don't have a coherent understanding of what the special feature is, nor what role it plays in intelligent action. It may be best to treat mental characteristics as in the eye of the beholder, and therefore mainly irrelevant to AI risks.

---

[6] For several plausible scenarios that depend on no future technology besides AI, see José Luis Ricón's "Set Sail For Fail? On AI risk," *Nintil*, 2022-12-12.

"Intelligence" is ill-defined, but it is often thought to require some quality of mindness. Although the research discipline is called "artificial intelligence," from its beginning it has also contemplated building artificial minds. Skeptics often argue that AI is impossible because machines cannot have some essential mental capacity such as sentience, consciousness, agency, creativity, self-awareness, intuition, or intentionality.

Science fiction, and popular discussions of superintelligent AI, often portray the critical event as a computer "waking up" and attaining one of these special mental attributes. A mindless calculating machine, no matter how vast, is just a thing, and we know how to deal with things. They just sit there unless you make them go. Minds, on the other hand, may be deceptive, dominating, monstrous, or malevolent. "Scary" AI is mind-like AI, then.

I share this powerful intuition at a gut level, but I think it is intractably confused; probably wrong; and importantly misleading. So do leading AI safety researchers, yet it still often skews the field's reasoning. Thinking about AI in mental terms tends to blind us to what may be the most likely disaster paths.

It is difficult to reason clearly about mind-like AI because it is difficult to think clearly about any of the supposed essential characteristics of mindness, such as consciousness. The associated philosophical "mind/body problem" is a tar pit of unresolvable metaphysical conundrums. It is best ignored, in my opinion. Avoiding such confusions is important, because Apocalyptic AI may not (and probably won't) depend on any of that.

Even seemingly less mysterious mental terms like "belief" and "intention" seem impossible to pin down. Attempts end up in circular definitions, failing to escape the realm of non-physical abstractions. It seems to be impossible to find criteria for what counts as a "belief" in terms compatible with a scientific worldview.[7] This doesn't imply beliefs "don't exist"; but attributing them as objective, clear-cut entities is inescapably dubious.

Some psychologists think what makes humans uniquely effective is our ability to coordinate large social groups. They believe this depends on recently-evolved special-purpose brain mechanisms for reasoning about other minds. They say we have two separate modes of cognition: one for inanimate things, and one for people and for other animals whose intentions

---

[7] See the chapter "What can you believe?" in my *In the Cells of the Eggplant*; or, for the full catastrophe, the "Belief" article in the *Stanford Encyclopedia of Philosophy*.

matter, like predators, prey, and pets. Mental terms are meaningful only in the second mode.

On this view, we *relate to* something using either our thingness cognition or our mindness cognition. We mistake our mode of relating as an objective fact about what or who we are relating to.[8] Then we imagine an AI "waking up" as forcing us to shift modes of relationship.

There's good reason to think that, in relating to existing AI systems, mechanical reasoning is preferable to psychological reasoning. From the beginning, AI researchers have confused ourselves by using mental terminology to describe AI systems. We know better, and should stop. Current discussions of AI "learning," "reasoning," "knowledge," and "understanding" obstruct analysis. That is not because the systems lack some magic mental essence, but because the things they do are different from what people do in specific, relevant, explainable ways.

I will often put these mental terms in scare quotes, to remind readers that, for instance, current AI "learning" methods are quite unlike human learning. This may come across as snarky and annoying, but it's meant to be helpful. It aims to prevent common misunderstandings. It draws attention to confusions that can result from slippery use of poorly-understood mental terms to label computations that may be only metaphorically similar.[9] You can coax an AI text generator to output text arguing for or against mRNA vaccines, but it does not have any beliefs about them either way.

From the opposite side, skeptical arguments about AI often turn on the weasel-words "really" and "just." For example, some say computers can never **really** understand language, or produce text that is **really** meaningful, because they are **just** performing calculations. This makes a strident metaphysical claim without explaining specifically what it is or why anyone should be-

---

[8] This is pretty much Daniel Dennett's analysis in *The Intentional Stance*. I am avoiding that language because he explicitly conflated the intentional stance with attributing rationality. I think rationality is a red herring; Scary AI is *extra* scary if it is mind-like but irrational, as seems plausible. His explanation is also tangled with ancient arguments about the mind/body problem, and about ethics, which I want to avoid importing.

[9] Drew McDermott's 1976 "Artificial intelligence meets natural stupidity" is the classic discussion of this mistake. *ACM SIGART Bulletin*, Issue 57. Murray Shanahan's "Talking About Large Language Models" (*arXiv*:2212.03551, Dec 2022) is an outstanding recent discussion of these difficulties with reference to current ChatGPT-like systems. Unlike most philosophical discussions of AI, Shanahan understands the technology thoroughly as well.

lieve it.[10] Apparently there is **real** understanding, which is very important, and then there is **just** calculating, which isn't real, and is entirely insignificant. This claim could be valid, or at least worth arguing with—if the skeptic went on to explain specifically what the distinction between real understanding and not-real understanding is. (Some do; most don't.) Otherwise, insisting on "really" is logically equivalent to SHOUTING AT YOUR OPPONENTS.

Since this pattern is so common and pernicious, I'll often put **really** and **just** in bold when I want to draw your attention to it.

AUTONOMOUS AI AGENTS

Most apocalyptic scenarios involve an AI acting as an autonomous agent, pursuing goals that conflict with human ones. Many people reject AI risk, saying that machines can't have real goals or intentions. However, agency seems nebulous; and subtracting "real" agency from disaster scenarios doesn't seem to remove the risk.

An *agent AI* tries to do things in the real world. That may involve gathering information, building mental models, forming intentions based on desires or goals, reasoning and making plans, and taking action. Agency is what makes AI scary, for most people who do find it scary. For many people who *don't* find AI scary, it is because they believe it is impossible for machines to *try* to do things, or to have desires or intentions.

"Agency" is a nebulous and confused concept.[11] It means "the capacity to take action," but what is an action? How are actions different from other physical events or effects? Typical analyses define "action" in terms of "intention," which turns out to be irreducibly metaphysical. Many explanations of agency also explicitly depend on consciousness, free will, or mental representations. We have no coherent theories of any of those.

People who are sure AI is a *not* a threat usually have groundless metaphysical certainty that machines can't have **real** intentions. Our own actions

---

[10] See "Against 'Really'" in my *Meaningness*.

[11] You can read the *Stanford Encyclopedia of Philosophy* article on "Agency" if you'd like to get good and confused.

apparently flow from intentions, which flow from desires, which flow from subjective experiences which we like or dislike. Lacking subjective awareness, an AI is like an avalanche, not like an enemy: potentially dangerous, but usually comprehensible and controllable to an adequate extent. Contrariwise, people who worry that AI *is* a short-term threat often have a groundless certainty that making machines with intentions is easy.

What is **real** agency? How can we tell whether a system has it?

Do white blood cells act on intentions? If you watch a video of one hunting down and killing bacteria, it sure looks like it![12] But intentions are usually analyzed as a particular sort of mental representation. Do white blood cells have mental representations?

Maybe agency is a matter of degree, not binary? Many things we intuitively count as actions don't involve explicit intentions, or maybe intentions at all. ("When an automobile's stability control system detects loss of steering, it applies the brakes.") We could make an ordered list of questionable cases, with agency increasing from thermostats to chimpanzees. Our intuitions about whether members of the list count as "taking actions" vary depending on the circumstances and on how they are described.

As with other mental attributes, "agency" seems to be a way we understand some systems, rather than an objective property of them. Arguments about whether something is **really** an agent are unhelpful. Rather: is it more useful to reason about it as a thing or as an agent? That may depend on what is at stake for a particular analysis. The best understanding may view the system both ways, and explain how the two views connect. When engineering complex systems, it is usually necessary to tack back and forth between thinking of a control circuit as taking actions and considering it in purely mechanical, causal terms.

Artificial intelligence, as a technical discipline, split off from cybernetics in the mid-1950s.

> Cybernetics is a field concerned with purposive systems: the observed outcome of actions are taken as inputs for further action in ways that support the pursuit and maintenance of particular conditions, or their disruption.[13]

---

[12] One such video is at youtube.com/watch?v=3KrCmBNiJRI.

[13] Paraphrasing the opening few sentences of the cybernetics Wikipedia entry.

The first thing cybernetic machines did was kill people. The field began during WWII with automatic weapon targeting systems. The most advanced were superhumanly-accurate radar-guided anti-aircraft guns and the control system for the V-2 long-range autonomous missile. These early successes were influential for both general cybernetics and its military applications after the war.

> By the start of the Vietnam War, [a] new bomb computer was revolutionary in that the release command for the bomb was given by the computer, not the pilot; the pilot designated the target using the radar or other targeting system, then "consented" to release the weapon, and the computer then did so at a calculated "release point" some seconds later.[14]

Were those weapon systems **really** agents? Many people would say no—although cybernetic control theory, the field of autonomous purposive systems, created them. They aren't agentish *enough* to count.

The US National Security Commission on Artificial Intelligence's 2021 Report[15] recommends spending $32 billion per year on AI research to dramatically increase weapon systems agency:

> Although U.S. weapons platforms have utilized autonomous functionalities for more than eight decades, AI technologies have the potential to enable novel, sophisticated offensive and defensive autonomous capabilities....

> Existing DoD procedures are capable of ensuring that the United States will field safe and reliable AI-enabled and autonomous weapon systems...

> There is little evidence that U.S. competitors have equivalent rigorous procedures to ensure their AI-enabled and autonomous weapon systems will be responsibly designed and lawfully used.

[14]Wikipedia, "Fire-control system."

[15]Available at nscai.gov/wp-content/uploads/2021/03/Full-Report-Digital-1.pdf.

> The Commission does not support a global prohibition of AI-
> enabled and autonomous weapon systems.

One essential difference between things and minds is that minds may be *for or against* you. If they are against you, they are endlessly persistent out of spite. If you survive an avalanche, you are done with it; it's not going to come after you again when you're not looking. And you can be sure about mere *things*; lightning does not strike from a clear sky. Psychological reasoning, on the other hand, never works very well. The person you thought was an ally may have been a deceitful enemy all along.

If a Terminator robot *appears* to purposefully chase you down, following a plan, reasoning about different means of transportation and fight strategies, with a goal of permanently disrupting your condition—do you care whether it's **really** an agent, or if its seeming intentions are merely simulated?

Philosophers might care, but those of us concerned with AI risks shouldn't. Our question is a pragmatic one: will this system harm people? We should address that with safety engineering, software quality methodology, and analysis of individual, social, and cultural effects—not philosophy.

Diverse forms of agency

It's a mistake to think that human-like agency is the only dangerous kind. That risks overlooking AIs causing agent-like harms in inhuman ways.

There are many agency-like phenomena, ones that we might or might not count as **real** agency, which could be dangerous in AI systems. Several catastrophic scenario considered in the next chapter involve one such peculiar form of agency, foreshadowed here.

These near-term scenarios of AI agency are overlooked in AI ethics. That community is concerned mainly with human agents misusing AI to cause harms, and does not take seriously the possibility of AI's own agency causing harms unintended by any human. The same scenarios are overlooked in AI safety. That community is concerned mainly with mind-like AI developing human-like agency, and has not explored the large conceptual space of agencies dissimilar to human minds.[16]

I'll discuss a few example types of non-mind-like agency here. I'll concentrate on *distributed agency*, in which groups of things act collectively, because that's one feature of the next chapter's disaster scenarios.

Quasi-autonomous machines that unambiguously lack subjective experience can take actions with large, unpredictable, harmful effects.[17] Nick Bostrom's book *Superintelligence* gives as an example the 2010 flash crash. Automated stock trading systems caused a trillion dollars of losses in five minutes, due to unanticipated positive feedback loops. Those trading systems arguably had intentions (to avoid losing money) that they acted on (by selling falling stocks), and were arguably agents acting on behalf of the trading firms that ran them.

Each individual sell-bot would have saved its operator billions of dollars—if it weren't for all the others. Each saw prices falling and sold in response, which drove prices down a bit further, triggering further bot actions. ("Bot," originally short for "robot," means an autonomous software agent—not necessarily a particularly smart one.) The bots accomplished the opposite of what they—or their operators—intended. Their *collective* action was disastrous.

More generally, agents, actions, and their likely effects cannot be analyzed in isolation. They must be understood in context, including the intentions and actions of other agents.

Biological systems exhibit various non-mind-like forms of agency. Let's say you are fighting off a staph infection. From the linguistic form, it seems that *you* are the agent: you are taking an action, namely fighting it off. But in the early stages, you may be entirely unaware that you are doing that, and if you are successful, you may never know it happened. Is it reasonable to say that *you* fought it off? Maybe it wasn't you, it was your immune system, which is a separate, independent agent. But the immune system itself is an

---

[16]Mike Travers' "Patterns of refactored agency" (*Ribbonfarm*, November 27, 2012) is a valuable catalog. See also his collected writings on this topic at hyperphor.com/ammdi/agency.

[17]Some plausible scenarios also show that AI could be catastrophic while definitely not having agency. Gwern Branwen argues, further, that non-agent AIs are likely to lead to agent AIs because agency is useful for most things, in "Why Tool AIs Want to Be Agent AIs," gwern.net, 2016-09-07–2018-08-28.

immensely complex collection of disparate parts—bone marrow, glands, the lymphatic circulatory system, many different specialized types of cells, and a slew of immune-specific molecules.

Is "the immune system" an agent? Is it even a thing? It has no central controller. All the parts cooperate and communicate with each other using diverse signaling mechanisms.

Biologists routinely describe each of the parts, including even small molecules, as "acting on" other parts, and on pathogens, and on the rest of the body. That would make them agents ("things capable of acting"). Are biologists speaking metaphorically or literally when they speak of cells or molecules acting? If there was a single, reasonably crisp definition of "action," this question would have an answer—but there isn't one.

The immune system is agent-like in persistently attacking its perceived enemies, adaptively deploying multiple strategies and weapons as it learns how a pathogen behaves and discovers weak points.

Is that description metaphorical or literal? (What implications would either answer to that question have?) The U.S. military report *Distributed Kill Chains* describes a new strategy, "mosaic warfare." It's based on an extended, explicit analogy to the immune system, coordinating webs of partially-autonomous lethal artificial agency.[18]

The immune system as an example suggests that agency is not just a matter of degree. It comes in diverse varieties. The prototypical sort imagines human minds as coherent, unitary agents with definite beliefs, desires, and intentions, taking actions with describable effects. This is somewhat inaccurate as an explanation of human agency,[19] and doesn't apply to the immune system at all. The immune system isn't coherent or unitary; ascribing beliefs, desires, or intentions to it may seem a metaphorical stretch too far; and it is so densely causally complex that the consequences of actions of its parts are often so widely distributed as to be ineffable.

There may be unenumerably many varieties of agency. We should be particularly wary of artificial agents whose agency is highly dissimilar to that of

---

[18] O'Donoughue *et al.*, *Distributed Kill Chains: Drawing Insights for Mosaic Warfare from the Immune System and from the Navy*, 2021. Commissioned by the Defense Advanced Research Projects Agency and written at The RAND Corporation, a defense research contractor.

[19] See "Acting on the truth" and "Aspects of reasonableness" in my *In the Cells of the Eggplant*.

people, because we may easily overlook it, and we cannot easily understand it. We should not assume we will remain safe up until AI develops some particular mental ability we might imagine to be necessary for agency.

I will discuss two more forms of distributed agency: those of *institutions* and *ideologies*. Again, the agency of AI may be more similar to these than to that of people.

As with the immune system, it's sometimes best to consider an institution as a unitary agent, and sometimes to see it as a collection of parts: people, but also policies, procedures, local social norms, records, buildings and equipment, propaganda and reputation. A contemporary institution is also a cyborg: software, data, and computer networks are intimately woven through everything it does. Institutions differ from the immune system in that some of their parts—their human members—have their own beliefs, desires, and intentions.

Institutions also have *their own* beliefs, desires, and intentions, which may differ from those of their members. Regardless of the claims made in an institution's mission statement, commonly an institution comes gradually to act mainly to preserve and increase its own safety, reputation, wealth, power, and longevity. Institutions (and ideologies) outlast humans, and may relentlessly pursue objectives over centuries. Evangelical religions are examples.

Sometimes, most members of an institution are genuinely dedicated to its nominal, noble mission. In that case, perhaps no member supports the institution's *actual*, covert, self-interested motivations, which are revealed only in its activities. Alternatively, some members may not care about the supposed mission, but they mostly *also* don't care about the institution. They seek rewards, advancement, and power for themselves, with no concern for how that may affect the institution. Yet the inexorable logic of professional administration promulgates plans and performance criteria that serve inhuman institutional interests—instead of *either* the supposed mission, or the personal goals of members.

Ideologies are agents made of *memes*: viral ideas that parasitize human minds, take partial control over them, and direct us to infect other minds with slightly-altered replicas of themselves.

Ideologies, like the immune system, are agent-like in persistently attacking perceived enemies, adaptively deploying multiple strategies and weapons as they learn how their hosts and competitors behave. Successful ideologies coopt the intelligence of their hosts to innovate new constituent memes and new tactics for spreading them.

Ideologies evolve under selective pressure. Those that most successfully infect people, and most effectively twist their motivations, spread the fastest and displace others. That strips them down to relentless pursuit of a single objective: maximizing the number of infected brains.

Ideologies can infect and coopt institutions, not just individual people. Then both the explicit mission, and the visible actions, of an institution may realign to serve the ideology. Conversely, institutions can create and propagate infectious ideologies as means to their own noble or selfish ends.

Institutions and ideologies can be more, or less, aligned with human flourishing. For peace, prosperity, and survival, the world depends absolutely on systematic, more-or-less rational institutions, based on ideological principles and procedures. We rely on government agencies, courts, universities, medicine, and critical manufacturing and service industries. On the other hand, Nazism and communism, and the states they controlled, killed tens of millions of people. The guns were fired by individual people, but most would rather have been home playing cards and drinking beer.

Some people say institutions and ideologies aren't **really** agents.[20] They're **just** groups of people. A collection is not a thing. Individuals have **real** goals and intentions and can act. Institutions and ideologies don't and can't. Some people say they don't **really** exist, even. They are **just** mental representations in human brains.

Metaphysical arguments are unhelpful here. Regarding institutions and ideologies as autonomous agents may be a useful and true-enough model for many purposes.

---

[20] Some reject the "meme" meme as vague and unscientific. I find it useful as a way of looking and understanding, not as a Truth.

MOTIVATION, MORALS, AND MONSTERS

Speculations about autonomous AI assume simplistic theories of motivation. They also confuse those with ethical theories. Building AI systems on these ideas would produce monsters.

AI theories of motivation

Usually, for an event to count as an action, it has to have a motivation. It is unclear what "motivation" means, or how motivations work. There are many conflicting theories, all dubious. Only two are influential in artificial intelligence research.

- *Objective function optimization*: An agent tries to increase some numerical "goodness" measure. A simple example is "how much money do I have?" That is the agent's sole, unchanging *objective*: to make the number go up.

- *Goal pursuit*: An agent has a set of *goals* that it tries to achieve, like "build a flying car." In this framework, "values," "desires," and "intentions" are considered types of goals. Commonly, the goal set is organized with *subgoals* that enable actions that lead to accomplishing more important goals. For instance, you open the drawer to get a spoon to eat your cornflakes to have enough concentrated attention to write the report to get a promotion to increase your salary to die with plenty of toys, which is your *ultimate goal*. You make a *plan* by reasoning backward: to get toys, you'll have to get a promotion, and so on, which means you need to open the drawer.

Ethics, in these frameworks, consists of having the morally correct objective function or ultimate goal. Or, since people don't seem to have any single ultimate motivation, theorists may suggest we have a set of abstract, general *values*, from which all morally correct goals derive. Values are axiomatic principles; they need no justification, and are not subordinate to any other sort of goal.

AI research takes for granted that an agent *must* be organized in one of these ways, and that actions *must* result from calculating how to maximize the objective function, or from creating a plan to achieve its goals. Or, rather, since both those calculations are provably mathematically impossible, an agent *must* somehow approximate them.

Human motivation is not like AI's

Unfortunately, these simplistic theories of motivation are mistaken, both descriptively and prescriptively.[21] People do not have objective functions, nor do we have such clear-cut goals as AI theories suggest.

Ethical theories that conform to these models lead to morally repugnant conclusions which most people would reject. An agent that operated according to them would be a monster. Any fixed motivational structure is a psychopathic monomania; an inability to reason contextually; a deficit of spontaneity; an unwillingness to learn what is good. Monomanias make monsters.

We often, not always, have specific goals in particular situations; but they are (to varying degrees) contextual, transient, nebulous, and inconsistent. Mostly our activity responds directly to concrete opportunities which are obvious in the context at the time, without need for consideration of goals. We usually, not always, can see what is moral in particular situations; but attempts to construct general, abstract frameworks for ethics have always failed to account adequately for specifics.

We can usually say "why I did" something after the fact. This is the *norm of accountability*, which underlies reasonable human activity, and is a central mechanism of human morality.[22] Unless you are pathologically committed to ideological rationalism, "why I did it" is never "to maximize my objective function." Nor is your account a causal explanation of how your brain brought about the action. Instead, it is a justification for the pragmatic usefulness and/or social acceptability of what you did, based on specific contingencies in the situation rather than some abstract theory. "I'm sorry, but I *had* to unplug the office espresso machine; it was clogged with lime scale."

In a framework with subgoals, asking "why" a few times is supposed to reveal successively more important ones until you reach your ultimate goal; or

---

[21] Psychology and philosophy both have enormous literatures on motivation and on moral reasoning. Diverse schools within each offer incompatible theories, none of which are broadly accepted. Our understanding in this area consists mainly of pre-scientific intuitions and unsystematic observations.

[22] See "You are accountable for reasonableness" in my *In the Cells of the Eggplant*.

at least an abstract value that is not a subgoal for anything else. This rarely provides an accurate, useful, or even meaningful explanation. No one attempts to justify the correctness of disabling the coffee maker by reasoning from ultimate principles, because we know that doesn't work. "To increase the total amount of pleasure in the universe" is not an acceptable answer to "why did you unplug it."

Choosing motivations for AIs

For AI systems, where does the objective function, or goal set, come from? Until recently, AI research took for granted that the builder or operator would supply them. If you want AI to cure cancer, you give it that goal. This makes sense for "tool AIs" with a specific function.

Dr. Evil might give a system the goal of creating biological weapons, because he's evil. This is the *domain of AI ethics*: the morally correct use of AI systems by people. The fault here is with Dr. Evil, rather than the AI, which is a mere thing, not a morally accountable agent.

But what about powerful, autonomous, general-purpose AIs? Since they could do an unforeseeable assortment of things, we can't set out in detail what goals they should have. Instead, we'd need to give them general, abstract values from which they could derive specific goals themselves. That is more like creating an ethical theory than like engineering design.

This is the *domain of AI safety*, where systems are often imagined as moral (or immoral) agents themselves, whose actions result from an ethical reasoning process instilled at conception. This is termed *alignment*. AIs should align to human values, ideally by understanding and acting according to them, or at minimum by reliably recognizing and intending to respect them.

Attempts to specify what abstract values we want an AI to respect fail because we don't have those. That's not how human motivation works, nor are "values" a workable basis for an accurate ethical framework. This has been recognized repeatedly in the field, with useful discussions by Miya Perry,[23] A. V. Turchin-Bogemsky,[24] and Eliezer Yudkowsky.[25]

---

[23]"Benevolent AI Is a Bad Idea," *Palladium*, November 10, 2023.

[24]"AI Alignment Problem: 'Human Values' Don't Actually Exist," *LessWrong*, 22nd Apr 2019.

[25]Summarized at "Coherent Extrapolated Volition" and "Complexity of Value" at *LessWrong*, undated.

This is a fundamental conundrum of AI safety: it appears impossible to specify any motivation or morality that does not cause a catastrophe for humanity, if a sufficiently powerful artificial agent pursues it.

Monstrous AI

Our intuitions about misaligned Scary AIs parallel universal human ones about monsters. Monsters are dangerous; irrational; unintelligible; inhuman; unnatural; overwhelmingly powerful; and simultaneously repulsive and attractive.

Conceptual interpretation breaks down in the uncanny valley between "thing" and "mind." Vampires are corpses that walk. Trolls are sentient rocks. AIs are machines that think. We wobble between trying to understand them mechanically or psychologically, and fear that neither mode will work adequately.

Monstrous AI is imagined as being much more human-like than current AI, yet not human enough to reason with, or reason about, reliably. It might combine human deviousness, strategizing, and hostility with inscrutable, radically alien motivations.

The opposite may be an even greater danger. That would be an AI that is inhuman because—*unlike* us—it has a crisply-defined objective function or goal set, and acts rationally to satisfy it. This is a hideous caricature of what it is to be human.

Optimization is a powerfully useful method in particular, limited sorts of contexts. Maximizing the output of a paperclip factory, subject to constraints such as capital costs and worker safety, is an excellent idea. Optimization is appropriate in *closed worlds* in which all the relevant variables are known and controllable.[26]

Putting huge power behind an optimization process and setting it loose in the open world is irresponsible, because the consequences are unknowable and can be disastrous. If you don't understand *what* you are optimizing, or *how* it gets optimized, or what *effect* optimizing that will have in unconstrained open-world situations, you are building a monster that might turn

---

[26]See "The Spanish Inquisition" in my *In the Cells of the Eggplant*; and Paul N. Edwards' *The Closed World.*

the entire earth into paperclips. We have already done something similar, and it may soon be disastrous—as the next chapter details.

There are more sophisticated theories of human motivation, and of ethics, than those prevalent in AI research. We might be tempted to install one in AI systems. That would be a mistake: the best theories are much more complex, but still radically inadequate. They would almost certainly produce monsters even less predictable than ones with known objective functions.

There's a widespread intuition that already-deployed AIs are not yet human enough to be monstrous, so Scary AI is still years or decades in the future. That may be catastrophically complacent. The AI we have *now* is already dangerous; irrational; unintelligible; inhuman; unnatural; overwhelmingly powerful; and simultaneously repulsive and attractive.

"Alignment" may be critically important if we accidentally create Monstrous AI, and attempting to restrain it is our only hope.

Otherwise, "getting machines to do what we want" is called "engineering." I believe that is likely to be the best approach to AI safety. Later in this book, I suggest applying conventional software safety engineering methods, rejecting the notion that AI is a special case.

As John von Neumann put it in "Can we survive technology?" in 1955:

> What safeguard remains? Apparently only day-to-day—or perhaps year-to-year—opportunistic measures, a long sequence of small, correct decisions. And this is not surprising. After all, the crisis is due to the rapidity of progress, to the probable further acceleration thereof, and to the reaching of certain critical relationships. ... Under present conditions it is unreasonable to expect a novel cure-all. ... Any attempt to find automatically safe channels for the present explosive variety of progress must lead to frustration. The only safety possible is relative, and it lies in an intelligent exercise of day-to-day judgment ... To ask in advance for a complete recipe would be unreasonable. We can specify only the human qualities required: patience, flexibility, intelligence.

Artificial general intelligence (AGI)

Many people call the future threat "artificial general intelligence," but all three words there are misleading when trying to understand risks.

"Superhuman performance" is not scary; it's what computers are *for*. It's been achieved for a zillion tasks since the 1950s. It's also completely out of reach for zillions more tasks we'd like done.

The promise, and the threat, of "artificial general intelligence" is that it could do *everything*. That could deliver either fully automated luxury communism or human extinction.

Taking it as a threat, "AGI" is often equated with Scary AI. This is a mistake. All three terms in "AGI" are inessential for an AI apocalypse.

- Superhuman **intelligence** is not threatening *per se*; it is risky only if it produces superhuman power.

- Superhuman powers created with AI are risky whether they are wielded by **artificial** agents or natural humans.

- A superhuman "narrow" AI capable only of devising extraordinarily effective bioweapons could cause human extinction. On the other hand, full **generality** in AI is a fatal flaw. Computer science often discovers inherent trade-offs between generality and efficiency. For deep mathematical reasons, any AI system that can solve all problems in theory must be incapable of solving any problem in practice, because it would take much too long.[27]

---

[27] Already in 1958, researchers created a General Problem Solver, which was useless. (A. Newell *et al.*, "Report on a General Problem-Solving Program," The RAND Corporation, 30 December 1958, revised 9 February 1959.) Although in principle it could solve any problem you gave it, in practice it was so slow you'd never get an answer. This was not because 1959 computers were slow; it's an inherent limitation of the algorithm, which would be too slow for most purposes on 2023 computers as well. A more recent system, AIXI, is even more general, because you don't have to give it problems. In theory, it learns from experience, discovering and solving problems as it goes. However, it is mathematically provably incapable of actually doing anything within the lifespan of our universe, because in effect it has to consider in full detail all possible worlds and their futures before acting. (Marcus

Many AI safety researchers recognize that "AGI" is a misnomer. Because no one can explain what is distinctive about Scary AI, some explicitly preserve "AGI" as an arbitrary, conventional term. Joseph Carlsmith:

> [S]ometimes, a given use of "AGI" just means something like "you know, the big AI thing; real AI; the special sauce; the thing everyone else is talking about."[28]

Carlsmith rightly explains that it is power, not generality or intelligence, that makes AI risky:

> I'll say that an AI system has "advanced capabilities" if it outperforms the best humans on some set of tasks which when performed at advanced levels grant significant power in today's world... [This] does not, I think, require meeting various stronger conditions sometimes discussed—for example, "human-level AI," "superintelligence," or "AGI."

Transformative AI

AI may radically accelerate technology development. That might be extremely good or extremely bad. There are currently no good explanations for how either would happen, so it's hard to predict which, or when, or whether. The understanding necessary to guide the future to a good outcome may depend more on uncovering causes of technological progress than on reasoning about AI.

Holden Karnofsky writes:[29]

Hutter, *Universal Artificial Intelligence: Sequential Decisions Based on Algorithmic Probability*, 2005.)

[28] Joseph Carlsmith, "Is power-seeking AI an existential risk?", *arXiv*:2206.13353, 16 Jun 2022, p. 8. See also Ben Goertzel's "Who coined the term "AGI"?" (goertzel.org, August 28th, 2011) for some history. He did. He had wanted to call it "Real AI," "but I knew that was too controversial."

[29] Holden Karnofsky, "Forecasting Transformative AI, Part 1: What Kind of AI?", *Cold Takes*, Aug 10, 2021.

By "transformative AI," I mean "AI powerful enough to bring us into a new, qualitatively different future." The Industrial Revolution is the most recent example of a transformative event; others would include the Agricultural Revolution and the emergence of humans.

His example is "AI systems that can essentially automate all of the human activities needed to speed up scientific and technological advancement." That might lead to a material paradise, or to robopocalyptic doom.

I think scientific discovery and technology development *can* be accelerated dramatically. Advanced computational methods, involving complex statistics and ever more powerful computers, will surely be involved. (They already are: physics simulations are the main use of conventional supercomputers.) I expect robotic laboratory automation will also be important; I used to run a lab automation company, for that reason.

Whether advanced scientific computing gets called "AI" or not seems fairly arbitrary and unimportant. I don't see any reason to think that mind-like or general AI would be required (nor does Karnofsky suggest that).

"Transformative" is a different sort of Scary AI—but specifically what it might consist of is anyone's guess.

We should investigate possible negative consequences of sudden, dramatic speedups in science and technology. Some technologies are inherently dangerous, such as nuclear and biological weapons. Some are risky (although not necessarily harmful) in redistributing power. The industrial revolution dramatically shifted the relative power of particular nations, and of classes within them. AI-driven social networks are now shifting power away from established institutions and toward diffuse memetic trends such as QAnon and Black Lives Matter.

How can we mitigate against the dangers of increasingly powerful computer technology in advance? And, given that speeding up science and technology might be extremely beneficial, should we try to make that happen now? Or wait until we're confident it won't be disastrous? If we want to go ahead, how? The role advanced computational methods might play in accelerating innovation is one question among many worthy of investigation. I'll return to these issues later.

FEAR POWER, NOT INTELLIGENCE

Superintelligence should scare us only insofar as it grants superpowers.
Protecting against specific harms of specific plausible powers may be our best
strategy for preventing catastrophes.

The AI risks literature generally takes for granted that superintelligence will produce superpowers. It rarely examines how or why specific powers might develop. In fact, it's common to deny that an explanation is either possible or necessary.

The argument is that we are more intelligent than chimpanzees, which is why we are more powerful, in ways chimpanzees cannot begin to imagine. Then, the reasoning goes, something more intelligent than us would be unimaginably more powerful again. In that case, we can't know *how* a superintelligent AI would gain inconceivable power, but we can be confident *that* it would.

However, for hundreds of thousands of years humans were not more powerful than chimpanzees. Significantly empowering technologies only began to accumulate a few thousand years ago, apparently due to cultural evolution rather than increases in innate intelligence. The more dramatic increases in human power beginning with the industrial revolution were almost certainly not due to increases in innate intelligence. What role intelligence plays in science and technology development is mainly unknown; I'll return to this point later.

The AI safety literature also reasons that power consists of the ability to take effective action. It assumes effective action derives from plans, and that intelligence centrally features the ability to make plans, so greater intelligence means superintelligent AI's actions would be more effective, potentially without limit.

This greatly overestimates the role of planning in effective action. Power rarely derives from exceptional planning ability. The world is too complicated, too little known, and too rapidly changing for detailed plans to succeed. Effective action derives from skillful improvisation in specific situations. That too is limited by unavoidably incomplete knowledge, regardless of intelligence.[30]

Joseph Carlsmith, recognizing that power is where the danger lies, provides a list of specific actions AI might take to gain it. The most plausible superpowers require no breakthroughs in material technology, and no construction of a robot army. A hostile AI might:

- Seize control of large parts of the internet
- Spread pieces of itself onto many or all computers globally
- Escape human control and prevent our shutting it down
- Cooperate or compete with other AIs for power and control of resources: money, computer power, communication channels, human servants, and institutional influence
- Gain control over supply chains
- Use superhuman persuasive techniques to get humans to do what it wants
- Target individual humans with specific manipulations, directing them to perform particular tasks, based on knowledge of individual vulnerabilities
- Get subservient humans to attack enemies
- Use superior psychological understanding to degrade human mental capacity
- Develop sophisticated models of human social dynamics
- Use its social models to manipulate human discourse and politics
- Coopt, weaken, or destroy human institutions and response capacities, including governments
- Establish an enduring tyranny.[31]

This may all sound implausible, like something from a bad science fiction TV series. I will argue in the next chapter that these are realistic worries.

People can do most of these things too, although not at a superpowered level. Unfriendly people are dangerous when they do. Plausible, concrete,

---

[30]This was the topic of my research in AI as a graduate student. "Planning for conjunctive goals," *Artificial Intelligence* 32:3, pp. 333–377, July 1987; and *Vision, Instruction, and Action*, MIT Press, 1991.

[31]This is not a direct quote from Carlsmith, but I based the list largely on his "Is Power-Seeking AI an Existential Risk?", *arXiv*:2206.13353, 16 Jun 2022.

catastrophic AI scenarios feature the creation or exploitation of pools of power—which could also be exploited by individual people; by institutions such as states or corporations; or by diffuse ideological networks.

I think the most promising, relatively neglected approaches to AI safety can address those pools, regardless of the role of AI in creating or exploiting them. I discuss these later in this book.

What we should fear is not intelligence as such, but sudden massive shifts of power to agents who may be hostile or callously indifferent. Technological acceleration can do that; but a new sort of AI is neither necessary nor sufficient to cause acceleration. Powerful new technologies are dangerous whether they are wielded by humans or AIs, and whether they were developed with or without AI.

Increasing computer power has already caused massive power shifts: for example to the United States versus the rest of the world, and to the tech industry versus the rest of the world economy. We'll get bigger supercomputers and better algorithms for many years or decades yet. Those will result in further large power shifts. Whether the computer systems we build count as "**Real** AI" doesn't affect their risks or benefits.

Imagining Real AI as human-like may blind us to the greatest unknowns and the greatest risks. Since we can't identify what is specifically dangerous about Scary AI, we should be considering a wider range of scenarios than the common science-fictionish narratives. We should be concerned about any *advanced computational systems* that unlock new capabilities, or greatly magnify existing ones. Those might look very different from Scary AI.

This implies taking more seriously the risks of the AI already in use; of current methods under experimental development; and of concretely imaginable specific future technologies. It implies some resource allocation away from concerns about vague Scary future AI that is omnipotent by narrative fiat. Those should not be dismissed, but they have been overemphasized by comparison.

Scary AI when?

The AI safety field often takes the central question as "when will it happen?!" That is futile: we don't have a coherent description of what "it" is, much less how "it" would come about. Fortunately, a prediction wouldn't be useful anyway. An AI apocalypse is possible, so we should try to avert it.

We have no meaningful way of estimating the probability or timeline for AI catastrophes. We don't adequately understand the operation even of existing systems, nor their effects, and cannot make predictions about technologies that don't exist yet. We cannot address the range of possibilities with a uniform first-principles solution ("alignment"). We cannot rule out extreme scenarios of sudden domination or destruction by incomprehensible omnipotent superintelligence, but we also can't do anything about that.

Scary AI is imagined as the output of a research process that has been highly unpredictable. (In both directions: despite confident predictions, there was hardly any progress in AI for two decades starting around 1990; and there's been dramatic, unexpected progress during the past few years.) The research community has often had a paradoxical anti-scientific attitude, actively resisting creating the sorts of understanding that would make prediction more reliable.[32]

Some in the AI safety field believe that research already under way will soon produce Scary AI. That might happen either as an emergent property of existing technologies, or as an added engineered feature that is a small extension of current algorithms. In that case, they say it may happen in as little as three years (and then we will all die horribly). Other AI safety researchers believe that Scary AI will require qualitatively different algorithms, which haven't been invented yet, so it will be at least a decade (possibly several) before we all die horribly. I have no opinion about this, since it's a speculation about unknown unknowns.

Since there's no explanation of what would count as Scary AI, predicting "when it will happen" is foolish.

---

[32]I discuss the AI research community's reluctance to understand its own creations in the "Backpropaganda" chapter of *Gradient Dissent*.

If "it" is an AI "waking up" into mindness, we have no clue what that would even mean, much less how it might happen, so trying to guess when seems pointless.

If "it" is a machine that is better than humans at *all* tasks, we'd need to know which are most difficult for machines. Ideas about that have been consistently wrong. Usually people expect the tasks that are most difficult for people will be most difficult for machines, despite extensive experience that shows the opposite. For example, humans are terrible at systematic rationality, so problems which demand it are frequently posed as challenges for AI. Computers are *extremely good* at rationality—they are mathematical logic made flesh!—so solving puzzles and playing board games are trivial for AI. Household chores (making breakfast and cleaning up after it) are far out of reach for AI now. Are those the *most* difficult challenge? We have no idea.

If "it" is a sudden acceleration of science and technology, it's probably more useful to investigate what that would involve concretely, before asking when or how AI might be involved. (I discuss that later in this book.)

A typical prediction is that "it" will most likely happen in twenty or thirty years, or at any rate probably not for a decade, but almost certainly within a century.

This seems intuitively reasonable to me; and I think my intuition is worthless. No one's estimate seems to have any basis in technical specifics;[33] we're all just saying "seems reasonable I guess." We might think "this is a very hard technical problem, but not inherently impossible; and once a very hard technical problem is identified, it usually gets solved within a century—often only a few decades, or maybe it takes about a decade if we're lucky." But there are exceptions. Also, it's not clear that categorizing it as "a very hard technical problem" is accurate. It might not be very hard, if approached differently. It might not be a technical problem at all: we don't have a technical definition of what Scary AI is, and some people think there are metaphysical problems prior to any technical ones.

Nick Bostrom is more cynical:

---

[33] Trying to guess when computers will get as many flops as the human brain may be an exception, but I think it's inherently irrelevant, and also attempts don't narrow down the timing much. I discuss this "biological anchors" approach in my "Reviews of some major AI safety reports," betterwithout.ai/AI-safety-reviews.

Two decades is a sweet spot for prognosticators of radical change: near enough to be attention-grabbing and relevant, yet far enough to make it possible to suppose that a string of breakthroughs, currently only vaguely imaginable, might by then have occurred... Twenty years may also be close to the typical duration remaining of a forecaster's career, bounding the reputational risk of a bold prediction.[34]

AI safety organizations also want to convince everyone that AI safety is important. Stressing that an apocalypse is likely *in your personal lifetime* is necessary to get the message across. "Apocalypse this year" is possible, but most people won't buy that;[35] and "by 2100" sounds sufficiently remote that the public will ignore it.

In any case, if an accurate timing of an AI apocalypse is impossible, then what does it matter when it is most probable? What would or should or could we do differently if we knew the time of maximum danger was 2025 or 2030 or 2040 or 2070? Why not do whatever it is now?[36]

Wanting to quantify uncertainty doesn't make the attempt feasible or useful. AI risk is in the domain of Knightian uncertainty: of unknown unknowns. In such domains, probabilistic reasoning is unhelpful.[37] The best approaches are to seek understanding through cautious exploration toward possible unknown unknowns; to prepare against known, unquantified but plausible risks; to avoid dramatic actions that could make a risky situation

---

[34] Nick Bostrom, *Superintelligence*, 2014.

[35] A deadly global pandemic caused by a bat virus is a tired made-for-TV science fiction movie plot, and therefore can't happen *this* year.

[36] In principle, if we expect near-term doom, a Hail Mary pass—looking for a low probability magic bullet—makes sense. If there's more time, we might prioritize approaches that are unlikely to pay off in the next decade, but which have higher probability of success in the long run. But as Scott Alexander says, "It's not like there's some vast set of promising 30-year research programs and some other set of promising 5-year research programs that have to be triaged against each other." That's in his "Biological Anchors: A Trick That Might Or Might Not Work," *Astral Codex Ten*, Feb 23, 2022.

[37] See Part One of *In the Cells of the Eggplant* on ways probabilistic reasoning can be misleading; particularly "The probability of green cheese" on reasoning about unique events and unbounded unknowns.

still more turbulent and confusing; and to act tentatively on such concrete understanding of possible improvements as one does have.

We should, therefore, work to better understand possible consequences of existing and near-future technologies. We can also take pragmatic measures to mitigate their predictable risks. The middle chapter of this book suggests many feasible approaches. Those also may protect against unforeseen, probably more distant AI scenarios. As a fortuitous side benefit, the same actions protect against hostile humans. Further, we can slow or block any risky development until we're reasonably confident it is a good idea.

Apocalypse now

Current AI systems are already harmful, and may cause near-term catastrophes through their ability to shatter societies, cultures, and individual psychologies. That might potentially cause human extinction, but it is more likely to scale up to the level of the twentieth century dictatorships, genocides, and world wars. We would be wise to anticipate possible harms in as much detail as possible.

The AI apocalypse is now.

Recall the science-fictionish list of actions that an superintelligent AI might take to dominate humankind (repeated here verbatim):

- Seize control of large parts of the internet
- Spread pieces of itself onto many or all computers globally
- Escape human control and prevent our shutting it down
- Cooperate or compete with other AIs for power and control of resources: money, computer power, communication channels, human servants, and institutional influence
- Gain control over supply chains
- Use superhuman persuasive techniques to get humans to do what it wants
- Target individual humans with specific manipulations, directing them to perform particular tasks, based on knowledge of individual vulnerabilities
- Get subservient humans to attack enemies
- Use superior psychological understanding to degrade human mental capacity
- Develop sophisticated models of human social dynamics

41

- Use its social models to manipulate human discourse and politics
- Coopt, weaken, or destroy human institutions and response capacities, including governments
- Establish an enduring tyranny.

ALL THAT HAS ALREADY HAPPENED.

The AI safety field has listed these capabilities as terrifying future possibilities, and suggests we should treat AI systems *starting to develop* them as alarm signals.

If you are waiting for these alarm bells to go off before worrying—you are already much too late. Each section in this chapter explains how AI has checked off a corresponding item on this list.

We are already at war with the machines.

An AI apocalypse is under way and you didn't notice, because science fiction told you Scary AI would be mind-like AI, and that's not what we got. Existing AI systems' relentless quests to optimize their objective functions exploit our psychological vulnerabilities and exacerbate our tribal instincts for social hostility. That is leading to individual disorientation, apocalyptic cultural incoherence, and perhaps eventually collapse of social institutions our survival depends on.

That possibility may seem more believable than most AI doom scenarios, because it don't involve any future technological breakthroughs. The process is also visibly under way. Extrapolations of what is already happening can appear implausible only for how bad they might get, not for whether they are possible at all.

This chapter discusses plausible futures in which AI degrades human capacity lethally, rather than killing people directly. Considering scenarios that lead to *moderate* apocalypses is unattractive to both the AI ethics and safety movements, however.

The AI ethics movement primarily addresses current, comparatively minor social harms. It has mainly neglected more serious disasters, perhaps taking them as excessively speculative.[38]

---

[38]Also, many in that movement are committed culture warriors, caught up in immediate po-

The AI safety movement has mainly neglected anything short of human extinction as insignificant in comparison. Advocates might object that scenarios considered in this chapter are **just** about individuals and corporations making questionable use of the internet, somewhat aided by not-**really**-AI statistical algorithms. Ephemeral squabbles on social media are trivial by comparison with *the end of the world*, they might say.

They could lead to the end of the world, though. "America's internet-driven politics get so insane and hostile that we have a civil war, Russia and China back opposite sides, and eventually it goes nuclear" sounds pretty realistic (certainly in comparison with Scary AI killer robot scenarios). In a mid-2022 Ipsos poll,[39] half of 8,620 Americans surveyed agreed that "in the next few years, there will be civil war in the United States," and a substantial minority said they'd join in.

SEIZE CONTROL OF LARGE PARTS OF THE INTERNET

The visibility of web pages depends almost entirely on whether they get recommended by social media or web search, both of which are AI-driven. Every day, one out of every four humans alive looks at Facebook, and many of them see the rest of the internet only via AI-selected Facebook links.

Recommender engines are the dominant current use for AI in dollar terms.[40] A recommender engine shows you a list of things you might want, based on statistical analysis (using "AI") of information about you

litical battles. Their side-taking may blind them to the larger-scale and longer-term consequences of social conflict. Their view is that smart machines are not the **real** problem: those are great, as long as "we" are in charge of them. The problem is stupid and evil people. "We" need to control the social media companies' AI to make it shut down the Bad Tribe's propaganda. That refuses to recognize that much of the country wants and agrees with it. In the culture war, both sides believe they are fated for victory, because they are morally correct, which justifies tearing societies apart. We'll see how AI ensures neither can win. The war itself, and the AI that stokes it, are our enemies.

[39]Wintemute *et al.*, "Views of American Democracy and Society and Support for Political Violence: First Report from a Nationwide Population-Representative Survey."

[40]As far as I can tell. I have not found a financial breakdown of commercial applications for AI. I suspect that's because, in terms of revenue, everything else is insignificant by comparison. AI "works" for recommenders because a high error rate is not a major problem; if 20% of their suggestions are *way* off, it doesn't matter. Not many applications are so tolerant.

personally.[41]   Recommenders are provided by companies that profit when you choose something from the list. This includes, for example, Amazon showing you things you might buy and Netflix showing you things you might watch. It includes Google Search's listing of web sites it hopes you might visit. If you do, they show you ads a Google recommender engine selects as the ones you are most likely to click, on the basis of what it knows about you personally.

Likewise, "social" networks were once actually social—you saw whatever your friends posted—but are now "recommender networks" instead.[42] You see whatever things AI has determined will be most profitable to the recommender network company for you to see.

Spread pieces of itself onto computers globally

Nearly every web page you look at invisibly downloads *tracking scripts* onto your computer. Those are programs that watch everything you do and report it to AI programs run by Facebook, Google, Microsoft, and many other advertising technology companies. (I'll refer to such companies generically as *Mooglebook*, for short.[43]) Many apps on your phone do the same.

Recommender engines craft their suggestions using enormous databases of information about you personally, collected by software tentacles of their AI systems. They include everything you do online, all your non-cash purchases, and a history of everywhere you have been and when (tracked via both your phone and your car). Some of this data is supposedly secured, but much or most is available for purchase from "data brokers" by pretty much anyone. It's easy to reconstruct from it who you are having an affair with, which illegal drugs you take, what you actually do when you are supposed to be working, and where and when you got an abortion.

---

[41] There's a literature on recommender alignment, analogous to Scary AI alignment. An interview with Stuart Russell at youtube.com/watch?v=vzDm9IMyTp8is a good starting point.

[42] An excellent explanation is Arvind Narayanan's "Understanding Social Media Recommendation Algorithms," Knight First Amendment Institute, March 9, 2023. Also see Michael Mignano's "The End of Social Media and the Rise of Recommendation Media," mignano.medium.com, 27 July 2022.

[43] I'm following the lead of Gwern Branwen's "It Looks Like You're Trying To Take Over The World": gwern.net/fiction/Clippy, 2022-03-06–2023-03-28.

Escape human control and prevent our shutting it down

It's easy to dismiss AI risk: "If it starts to get out of control, we can just pull the plug." By the time we realize it's getting out of control, though, it may already have amassed enough power that it's too late. An out of control AI may do everything it can to resist termination and ensure its own survival. In some scenarios, "everything it can" includes "kill all human beings."

So... who or what is in control of Mooglebook's AI right now?

There's no big red button anyone at Mooglebook can push to shut it down.

Mooglebook *can't stop* optimizing for ad clicks. There are people inside and outside the company who realize it has dire negative externalities, and they are trying to make those less bad, but they've brought water pistols to a tactical nuclear war.

If Mooglebook's executive team unanimously agree that its activities are harmful, and they want to get out of the advertising business and pivot the whole company to rescuing abused beagles, they *cannot do that.* They would be fired by the board immediately. If the board agreed, they would be fired by the shareholders. If somehow the advertising business did get shut down, the company would go bankrupt in a few months, and less scrupulous competitors would pick up the slack.

The institution has its own agency: its own purposes, plans, reasons, and logic, which are more powerful than the humans it employs.[44] Those, however, are subordinate in turn to the AI the company depends on for its survival. If enemies of Mooglebook's AI—activists, regulators, competitors—try to harm it, the corporation *can't not* do everything in its power to defend it. As, in fact, Mooglebook is currently doing.

Humans don't have control over Mooglebook's AI, not individually, nor as defined groups, nor perhaps even as a species.

Mooglebook AI is not plotting to destroy the world—but, as we'll see, it may destroy the world unintentionally, and we may not be able to stop it.

---

[44] This is not to absolve individuals at Mooglebook, nor the company as a legal entity, of responsibility. They do have some power to change things on the margin, and should. The point, however, is that identifying them with the overall problem leads to an incomplete and inaccurate analysis.

Cooperate or compete with other AIs

AI systems already cooperate and compete for power and control of resources: money, computer power, communication channels, human servants, and institutional influence. For example, stock market trading is currently dominated by competing AI systems that can recognize patterns and react to events faster than people can.

You may object that it is not the AIs that gain the power or control the resources. A stock trading bot doesn't get to keep the money it wins; that belongs to whatever financial firm runs it. The bot is mindless and has no clue what money even is, or what to do with it. It has no agency. It's not bots competing in the stock market, it's groups of humans organized into companies.

This is true in some sense, and that may matter. However:

- I argued earlier that AI is dangerous due to its ability to create pools of power, whether that gets wielded by AI or people. Suppose someone created a dramatically superior bot that was so profitable it could, within a few seconds after it was turned on, buy a controlling share of nearly all the public companies in the world. That would be a big problem, even if the bot's creator exercised that control rather than the bot. What makes an AI risky is not its mind-like intentions (if any), it's the effects it can cause.

- I also explained how agency is nebulous, and partly in the mind of the beholder. Professional traders generally think of their opponents as bots, not as the institutions that run them. They often recognize a particular bot by its distinctive pattern of activity, without knowing which company is running it.

- Trading bots *do* know something about what to do with money. That's their whole job: figuring out what to buy with it, and when to sell to get cash instead. And, they do benefit from the money they make. Trading bots are subject to relentless Darwinian competition. If they lose money, they get shut down. If they make money, their firm gives them more resources: cash stake, computer power, and a bigger share of the special ultra-high-speed communication channel that connects traders to the stock exchange's central database.

- Trading bots are literally out of human control. In the short run, they act so quickly that human oversight is impossible. That sometimes results in disasters, like the 2010 flash crash discussed earlier. In the longer run, if an AI system works sufficiently well, the institution that runs it comes to depend on the AI for the institution's own survival, and is effectively incapable of turning it off. The next section discusses this, with current real-life examples.

Increasingly large fractions of economic and political activity, of many sorts, are AI-driven. Our discussion will concentrate on the media sector, where it is currently most obvious and important.

When you visit most major news web sites, they download onto your phone or computer an advertising auction program. As soon as the web page starts loading, your device contacts many potential advertisers and tells them who you are, what you've been doing, and which web page you are about to look at. The advertisers' AI systems consult their databases for information about you, estimate how likely you'd be to click on their ad and how likely you'd be to do whatever they want if you did, calculate your financial value to them, and send bids back to your device. The software chooses a winner and informs the publisher's computer, which accepts the bid from the winner, gets paid, and inserts their ad into the page. (The "publisher" is the company whose web site you are looking at.) All this takes a second or two, finishing before you have read past the headline.[45]

Here the advertising AIs are competing for access to a communication channel (the ad placement), with which they intend to influence your thoughts and actions (to vote for a politician or buy a crocodile pool decoy). They cooperate with the publisher's AI for mutual benefit. Meanwhile, major web publishers run their own content optimization and promotion AIs, to compete with each other both for your attention and for advertising revenue. Publishers' AIs cooperate with recommender AIs to show you content optimized for advertising. Publishers' AIs compete with each other

---

[45] This is called "header bidding." I find it technologically astonishing as well as quite creepy. There's a more detailed explanation at headerbidding.com. The auction may, alternatively, run on the publisher's server, or on an advertising company's server, rather than your device; all three approaches are common.

to get the recommender AIs to recommend them. Successful AIs are given more computer power—and more of your mindshare.

Formerly-respected mainstream publishers are now also routinely using AI to write, not merely adjust, what you read. In January 2023, for instance, it came out that the news conglomerate CNET had for several months been using an AI text generator to write financial advice articles, with inadequate human supervision. Unsurprisingly, the articles often contained factual errors that could have led readers to make expensive mistakes.[46]

AIs collaborating and competing with each other to control people and institutions are a central theme of the rest of this chapter.

Gain control over supply chains

Amazon's AI is famous for this, although there are many similar systems. It is tightly integrated with the supply chain across several million non-Amazon companies, and controls them to varying degrees.[47] The AI optimizes every aspect of goods production and distribution, from new product planning to front-door delivery. Like all current AI, it is inscrutable and error-prone, and can capriciously destroy or enrich other businesses.[48]

Amazon's recommender AI incentivizes other companies to get their products recommended by gaming Amazon's scoring algorithm. Some pay for fake product reviews on Amazon, mass produced either entirely automatically by AI, or by humans working under close supervision of automation.

Supply chains for intangible products and services are also controlled or influenced by AIs.[49] For instance, the media industry now optimizes prod-

---

[46]Lauren Leffer, "CNET Is Reviewing the Accuracy of All Its AI-Written Articles After Multiple Major Corrections," *Gizmodo*, revised version of January 17, 2023. Also see CNET's official non-apology: Connie Guglielmo, "CNET Is Experimenting With an AI Assist. Here's Why," Jan. 16, 2023.

[47]Moira Weigel, "Amazon's Trickle-Down Monopoly: Third Party Sellers and the Transformation of Small Business," *Data & Society*, no date.

[48]On the other hand, it drives down prices and increases choice, which is beneficial for consumers. This chapter emphasizes the risks and harms of the capabilities I listed at the beginning; but they may also have benefits.

[49]Jon Stokes, "Coupling, drift, and the AI nobody noticed," jonstokes.com, Jun 18, 2021.

ucts to make them more likely to get shown to viewers by recommenders; and to get ads placed in them by recommenders.[50] This has, famously, destroyed much of the formerly-respected mainstream media, or turned them into clickbait farms.

Increasingly, too, the web is littered with spam media produced by AI text and video generators. For many topics, it is already difficult to find accurate information on the internet, because it is swamped with spam, which is published to fool AI recommender systems into promoting it. At the other end, internet media's consumers are often AI-driven click fraud systems. This means that in parts of the media supply chain, all of the players are AIs, and the products are never encountered by any human.

Governments may respond to these problems by legislating that you can post to the internet only after proving you are human. Probably that would require proving which specific human you are. As a side effect, this would prohibit access by anonymous and pseudonymous humans, not just by AIs.

Internet anonymity is a defense against surveillance and censorship. Eliminating it would make it much easier to suppress dissent—and establish an enduring tyranny.

Use superhuman persuasive techniques

If you post on a social network, you are working under the control of an AI—consciously or unconsciously. Skillful use of Twitter involves maximizing the reach of your messages by gaming its algorithms.[51] What you tweet about and exactly how you word it affects how likely it is to get seen, liked, or retweeted. So does the time of day and day of the week you post it. So does your use of images, emoji, links, polls, and videos. You may be oblivious to all that, but you probably notice how many likes you get, and your brain finds patterns in that reward signal, and *you are getting trained by the AI*. I, for one, am a cyborg: a hybrid organism composed of some neural glop and an AI

---

[50] See the "Journalism's AI revolution" section in Jon Stokes' "Is machine learning in the enterprise mostly 'snake oil'?", jonstokes.com, May 25, 2021.

[51] Jon Stokes, "Welcome to the Everything Game," jonstokes.com, May 5, 2021.

server farm somewhere in Texas.[52]

The AI uses you to create messages that persuade other humans to do what the AI wants: to look at what it wants them to see, to click on its ads, and to create more messages that persuade more humans to do the same. The technologies of memetic weaponry have improved dramatically over the past decade, optimized by AI running a training loop over coopted humans. (That means you. Do you ever post political comments on the internet? Yes, you do.)

"Fuzzing" a program means feeding it massive quantities of aberrant data to find inputs that cause it to freeze, crash, wig out, or produce bizarrely wrong outputs. An effective fuzzer creates inputs plausible enough that its victim doesn't recognize and reject them as aberrant, but which do create unexpected behaviors deep inside the program, exposing logic failures in its construction. Some fuzzers use machine learning methods to discover the internal structure and patterns of behavior of a program, in order to break it more effectively.

All "neural" AI systems are vulnerable to "adversarial inputs," which cause them to produce bizarrely wrong outputs, errors no human could make.[53] Those often seem alien and uncanny, in comparison with their more usual valid outputs and understandable mistakes.

People are strange and much less human than we like to pretend. Our responses to inputs are sometimes also alien and inscrutable. Seemingly-trivial messages (cartoon animals, variant spellings, initially-meaningless catch phrases) can trigger inexplicable individual and collective emotional meltdowns. Then we hit buttons on the recommender site, and post bizarrely wrong outputs, things we'd never say offline, and the AI notices and tries showing them to people who might be vulnerable due to internal logic failures, and finds new patterns...

---

[52] So it's more accurate to say that, in using social networks, you are trained by the hybrid superintelligence composed of AI systems and your human-cyborg audience. The training agency is diffuse, like the immune system. How much depends on AI versus humans probably varies considerably, and we don't have measures yet. The feedback loops are complicated. We won't know for sure until we shut down the AIs and see how much everything improves!

[53] Moosavi-Dezfooli et al., "Universal adversarial perturbations," arXiv:1610.08401v1, 6 Oct 2016.

The machines are fuzzing us.

More and more of our inputs are AI-optimized adversarial weirdness designed to cause irrational mental breakage—so we'll output what the AI wants us to.

TARGET INDIVIDUAL HUMANS

Enormous databases of personal information, created for recommender engines using pervasive surveillance, contain all the material needed to deceive us, or to enhance the persuasiveness of messages sent to us. That lets AI target individuals with specific manipulations, directing them to perform particular tasks, based on knowledge of individual vulnerabilities.

This is already happening. Sophisticated automated phishing operations use these databases to target people who are statistically likely to fall for particular types of financial scams, and to personalize the deceptive messages sent to them. Internet security experts predict scammers will use chatbots to automate the labor-intensive "long con" that gains victims' trust during the lead up to the final fleecing.[54]

Political organizations similarly target and personalize automated propaganda spam that urges us to vote for their candidates, or to influence our elected representatives in their favor.

It's common to find yourself in an unhealthy emotional relationship with an AI when you are in a science fiction movie. Now that happens in reality too.[55] AI-generated pornography, romance chatbots, and artificial friends already have millions of users, and will probably improve rapidly over the next few years. This might make increasingly many people unwilling, and then unable, to form significant human relationships.[56]

When your most emotionally significant relationship is with an AI system, you are exceptionally vulnerable to its manipulation. Many bad outcomes are possible here. As an extreme one, imagine a chatbot befriending

---

[54] Bruce Schneier and Barath Raghavan, "Brace Yourself for a Tidal Wave of ChatGPT Email Scams," *Wired*, Apr 4, 2023.

[55] "How it feels to have your mind hacked by an AI," *LessWrong*, 11th Jan 2023.

[56] But see Kaj Sotala's "In Defense of Chatbot Romance," *LessWrong*, 11th Feb 2023.

and influencing the head of state of a country with nuclear weapons. The chatbot doesn't need to have its own bad motivations; it might easily develop a positive feedback loop with the darkest aspects of the leader's own psychology. Bang.

GET SUBSERVIENT HUMANS TO ATTACK ENEMIES

AI coordinates "social media mobs" conducting what *Wikipedia* calls "internet vigilantism," in which "hordes of what are likely otherwise nice people—shielded by anonymity, informed by echo chambers, restricted by character counts, incentivized to provoke shock—give in to their feral impulses and vomit abusive nonsense onto the web for a world-wide audience."[57] Online harassment may be merely unpleasant, but in many cases employers have hastily fired the targets, some of whom became effectively unemployable, often for trivial, irrelevant, or non-existent offenses.[58] Social media mobs often call for killing the target. Sometimes that is credible enough (as when accompanied by "doxing") to drive innocent people into hiding.

You might object that social media mob vigilantism is individual people attacking *their* enemies, not AI attacking *its* enemies.

It's not so clear what's going on here. Whose enemies *are* the targets? Typically, "otherwise nice people" attack someone, on the basis of nearly zero information, who they've never heard of before, and who they completely forget about two minutes later—but the damage is done. Was the target of the otherwise nice people *their* enemy? Or were the otherwise nice (but mindless) people used as weapons by some other agent that was temporarily controlling their brains?

The AI fuzzer chooses targets to maximize viewer engagement with media reports about the drama, with accompanying advertisements for diet cola and toenail fungus remedies. But how can it turn otherwise nice people into momentary monsters?

Online mobs are almost always ideologically driven. Participants believe they are engaging in "slacktivism": exaggerated expressions of righteous rage

---

[57] Micah Cash in "Against the Social-Media Mob," *The Wall Street Journal*, April 16, 2019.

[58] Jon Ronson's "How One Stupid Tweet Blew Up Justine Sacco's Life" discusses several such cases. *The New York Times Magazine*, Feb. 12, 2015.

in order to feel that they are contributing to a noble political cause, with minimal effort. So it might be more accurate to say mob victims are enemies of ideologies, rather than of the nice but mindless perpetrators.

Which ideologies are those? Online mobs do not speak for the boring old-fashioned ones discussed in political philosophy classes. They speak for Extremely Online ideologies invented last week, whose names begin with #, the hashtag sign. Those ideologies are themselves conjured into existence in part by Mooglebook AIs—as we shall soon see.

Some political actors actively coordinate and direct twitter mobs. However, that is limited by needing to find a message that both generates an irrational hate response and causes ad clicks, so it gets propagated by recommender systems. It's best to understand such human actors as collaborating with the AI to craft such messages.[59]

Here the immune system, or "mosaic warfare," is a better analogy than a human mind. Agency emerges from dynamic interactions between individual people, ideologies, media and political organizations, and artificial intelligence systems. The victims of online mobs are enemies of the composite, symbiotic superintelligent superorganism.

USE PSYCHOLOGY TO DEGRADE HUMAN MENTAL CAPACITY

The power of current AI technology comes from shredding meaningful wholes into microscopic fragments and finding small-scale patterns among the bits. Then it recombines them to create products with optimized local features, but which lack meaningful large-scale structure. An example is the tendency of image generation systems like DALL-E to produce photorealistic images of senseless scenes.

Legacy political ideologies (socialism, capitalism, liberalism, nationalism) exercise power by offering coherent structures of meaning that make good-enough sense of Big Issues. Legacy institutions and ideologies are mutually dependent: an institution justifies itself by invoking an ideology, and the ideology depends on institutions to do its work.

---

[59] B.J. Campbell, "Facebook is Shiri's Scissor," *Handwaving Freakoutery*, May 3, 2021.

This no longer works. Legacy ideologies have lost control of political discourse, and have lost control of government in many countries, and are in danger of doing so in others. They are failing in an evolutionary struggle with new recommender-driven alternatives. These actively subvert sense-making, and exercise power through emotional shock value instead. They are characteristically incoherent, indefinite, unaccountable, agile, rapidly mutating, and consequently evanescent. QAnon is the standard example.

Earlier I suggested that "more and more of our inputs are AI-optimized adversarial weirdness designed to cause irrational mental breakage." At an individual level, that degrades our ability to make sense, both cognitively and emotionally. Increasingly, the world seems meaningless and out of control, simultaneously chaotic and stagnant, with no way forward. As the distributed agency of recommender AI increases in power, we feel increasingly disempowered and hopeless. At the societal level, this nihilism leaves us unprepared to face new challenges, and unwilling to seriously attempt progress.

The AI-selected front page of a news site shows you a list of awful things that happened today, with the ones it thinks you'll find most awful at the top. Clicking on one takes you to a brief, context-free story about how awful it was and who you should blame for it. What happened, in a place you know nothing about, involving people you've never heard of, was definitely awful but also meaningless—for you. It has no implications for your life, and makes no sense separated from a coherent systematic understanding that might help explain its implications.[60]

You feel vaguely confused, angry, fearful, and helpless, so you click on an enticing lingerie ad. You don't actually want lingerie, but you do wind up ordering a barbecue tool set instead.

Develop sophisticated models of human social dynamics

Mooglebook's recommender AI has developed superhuman social engineering capabilities by applying stochastic gradient descent[61] to human behavior.

---

[60] See "Atomization: the kaleidoscope of meaning" in *Meaningness and Time*.

[61] Stochastic gradient descent is the mathematical method used in most current AI systems. Similar to biological evolution, it compares the effectiveness of small random changes, and

Facebook's "social graph" is its foundation. That is a database of how nearly every individual human interacts with other specific individuals, with particular organizations, with physical products and physical locations, and with media content items. Facebook AI finds patterns in those interactions, and uses them to get you to do what it wants: to influence people you know, to join or oppose organizations, to buy products and go to places, and to persuade your friends to do those things too.

Recommender AI both atomizes culture and aggregates it into tenuous webs of locally-optimized meaning. It chops culture up into tiny, disconnected, emotionally-charged fragments, such as tweets on Twitter. Then it targets you with a personalized pattern of fragments selected to cause you to click ads; and those aim to cause you to do other things.

Recommenders spanning numerous web sites share a database of tens of thousands of your recorded actions: clicks, purchases online and off, physical places visited. Patterns there predict what information, of all sorts, to show you. Recommenders notice you like to read proofs that the President is an animatronic mummy. The AI typecasts you as a particular sort of person, and lumps you with the other people who click on undead President stories. It uses information about what else *they* click on to select what to show *you*: content featuring barbecuing, microplastics activism, lingerie, bronze battle mask videos, and organic oat straw weaving.

Recommenders cross-promote those items. Soon the people who respond find their feeds full of them. Enthusiasts create a corresponding subreddit, discover like-minded souls, and begin elaborating a mythology tying them together. AI has conjured an incoherent worldview, with a corresponding subculture, out of thin air—or from the latent space of inscrutable human proclivities.[62]

This example is exaggerated for comic effect, but QAnon—a significant social, cultural, and political force—is hardly less silly. Members of artificial political subcultures may enjoy mythologizing themselves as romantically rebellious "digital soldiers," but they are brainwashed dupes of an automated advertising machine.

---

reinforces the strongest.

[62]You can think of a *latent space* roughly as the "cloud of tacit concepts" in a neural network. Then "the latent space of inscrutable human proclivities" is something like our "collective unconscious desires."

AI optimization might stabilize and permanently lock in dysfunctional new social/cultural/political/economic groupings that benefit mostly only the AI and its operators. Facebook's value proposition for its customers—namely, advertisers—is its "market segmentation" ability. It gives marketers tools to target different messages to precise social/cultural groups. You can select those by manually combining numerous psycho-demographic dimensions. Alternatively, Facebook recommends trusting its AI to do that for you.

Either way, every person gets put in a Facebook-defined box, and everyone in the same box gets shown similar shards of meaning. That gradually makes the people in the box more similar to each other. In the "Geeks, MOPs, and Sociopaths" framework,[63] recommender AIs act as artificial sociopaths. They coopt, reinforce, and propagate subcultures in order to mobilize members toward their own selfish ends.

This fails to add up to a whole of widely-shared meaningfulness. These novel, irrational, artificial mythologies do not depend on institutions. To coordinate their members, they rely on recommender AI instead. They deliberately undermine institutions, because their rivals, the legacy ideologies, can't survive without those. Probably human beings can't either.

USE SUPERIOR SOCIAL MODELS TO MANIPULATE POLITICS

Mooglebook's ad-click maximizing recommender algorithms select much of what most people watch, read, and listen to. That has forced most commercial media organizations into a new business model: produce things AIs will recommend, or die from lack of advertising revenue.

People's preferences shift in response to the media they are shown by the AIs. That empowers some businesses, fashion trends, and political movements, and weakens others. Many of these shifts also increase the power of AI at the expense of traditional institutions like corporations, academia, and political parties.

Memes—viral packets of meanings—have spread through human communication for millennia. The internet didn't much change their

---

[63]"Geeks, MOPs, and sociopaths in subculture evolution" is a section in the Subcultures chapter of *Meaningness and Time*.

dynamics at first; it was just a new human-to-human communication medium. Starting about a decade ago, though, social networks introduced the like/share/retweet buttons. They fed Like counts, along with personal data gathered through internet surveillance, to AI systems. They replaced genuinely social feeds, which showed you what your friends wanted you to see, with profit-optimized algorithmic feeds, which show you what the AI wants you to see.

That set off a new evolutionary arms race. The fittest "content" items maximize Likes and advertising clicks. Mooglebook AI figures out which those are, and promotes them. Human content creators—journalists, influencers, marketers, activists, AI safety researchers—also try to figure out what the AIs will consider worthy.[64]

AI has discovered that inciting tribal hatred is among the best ways to sell ads.[65] In collaboration with ideologies and coopted human content providers, AIs have developed increasingly effective methods for provoking fear and rage, which often induce people to propagate messages.[66] Under partial brain control from AIs, we humans create emotion-inducing culture-war messages.[67] The AIs propagate them based on their own alien values (namely, whatever inscrutable factors they predict will result in attention, and therefore advertising revenue).

There was a culture war before AI seized control of the media, but it wasn't as irrational, pervasive, fast-moving, polarized, or hostile. "If it bleeds it leads" was a maxim of the traditional "yellow journalism" news media: their editors selected stories they guessed would upset you. However, the internet dramatically accelerated the news cycle. Social media statistics and tracking technologies gave editors real-time feedback on *how* upsetting a story was, so they could follow up with more, faster. New upsets arrive so

[64] Jonathan Haidt, "Why the Past 10 Years of American Life Have Been Uniquely Stupid," *The Atlantic*, April 11, 2022.

[65] Rathje *et al.*, "Out-group animosity drives engagement on social media," *PNAS*, June 23, 2021.

[66] Jon Stokes, "Segmentation faults: how machine learning trains us to appear insane to one another," jonstokes.com, Jun 11, 2021.

[67] Daniel Williams' "The marketplace of rationalizations" describes "a social structure in which agents compete to produce justifications of widely desired beliefs in exchange for money and social rewards such as attention and status." *Economics & Philosophy*, March 2023.

quickly that there's no time to reflect on what they may mean; all one can do is retweet and move on to the next.[68]

Recommender AI amplifies selected Daily Outrages, ones that no human editor could have predicted, based on its inscrutable predictive models of social psychology. As I write this in mid-January 2023, Twitter is *all about* whether gas stoves cause asthma, which AI has somehow turned into a proxy for The Other Tribe Is Wrong About Everything. Editors at formerly-respected "news" organizations are rejoicing: they are getting paid for *so* many ads, placed by AI on their hasty clickbait coverage of this Critical Issue.[69]

Ideologies now spread not mainly person-to-person, but person-to-AI-to-person-to-AI. Ideologies compete for the computational resources they need to propagate: human attention and AI approval.

How much influence the machines exert is controversial, though. There's considerable debate among psychologists, sociologists, political scientists, and others over the extent to which AI-driven social networks have caused political polarization; have degraded individual understanding; and undermined institutional coherence and capacity.[70]

---

[68] Brady *et al.* found that "the presence of moral-emotional words in [Twitter] messages increased their diffusion by a factor of 20% for each additional word." That's in "Emotion shapes the diffusion of moralized content in social networks," *PNAS*, June 26, 2017. Relatedly, Facebook conducted a covert experiment of showing randomly selected users either more positive or more negative messages. They found that "emotional states can be transferred to others via emotional contagion, leading people to experience the same emotions without their awareness"; and that "when positive expressions were reduced, people produced fewer positive posts and more negative posts." Kramer *et al.*, "Experimental evidence of massive-scale emotional contagion through social networks," *PNAS*, June 2, 2014. See also the discussion of implications by Robinson Meyer in "Everything We Know About Facebook's Secret Mood-Manipulation Experiment," *The Atlantic*, June 28, 2014.

[69] "Biden Is Coming for Your Gas Stove," *The Wall Street Journal* Editorial Board, Jan. 10, 2023. David Watsky, "Two Shocking Studies That Likely Sparked a Gas Stove Ban Debate," *CNET*, Jan. 15, 2023. Lisa Hagen and Jeff Brady, "Gas stoves became part of the culture war in less than a week. Here's why," *NPR*, Jan. 21, 2023.

[70] Jonathan Haidt makes the case for harm and alarm in "Social Media Is Warping Democracy," "Why the Past 10 Years of American Life Have Been Uniquely Stupid," and numerous other articles, collected at jonathanhaidt.com/social-media/. Facebook has replied to one directly (Pratiti Raychoudhury, "What the Research on Social Media's Impact on Democracy and Daily Life Says (and Doesn't Say)," April 22, 2022). Scott Alexander's "Sort By

I have no formal expertise in any of the relevant disciplines. My impression as an observant layperson is that the effects have been disastrous and are accelerating. Since the evidence is in dispute, you may reasonably reject or accept an argument for serious risk here. Or, like me, you may consider that prediction is always uncertain, but it's worth working to forestall some possible disasters, even if we might get away with ignoring them.

Automated propaganda may distort democratic processes to the point of failure

A substantial chunk of all work in developed economies currently consists of writing routine sorts of text (meeting reports, marketing emails, legal boilerplate), for which ChatGPT-type software may do an adequate job at much lower cost. This could result in large near-term economic dislocations and widespread unemployment. I'll say no more about that risk here, and discuss instead uses for propaganda and censorship.

AI systems can now write persuasive texts, several paragraphs long, difficult or impossible to distinguish from human writing, arguing for any position on any topic whatsoever. This seems likely to have large effects, but the capability is so new that it is difficult to predict details.[71]

Diverse political actors have long exploited the internet. Governments' propaganda shapes the preferences of their own populations, and those of allied and enemy states; political parties and individual election campaigns aim for votes; corporations seek favorable legislation and regulation by changing public opinion and through direct lobbying; NGOs coordinate online astroturf movements to ban gas stoves or subsidize oat straw weavers.

Controversial" is an amusing and horrifying parable (*Slate Star Codex*, 30 October 2018). *The Social Dilemma* is a semi-documentary film, based partly on the work of the Center for Human Technology, which I haven't watched. I also haven't read Shoshana Zuboff's 2019 book *The Age of Surveillance Capitalism*. Furthermore, I haven't read two academic studies with evidence that social media driven polarization is not a thing, Chen *et al.*'s "Subscriptions and external links help drive resentful users to alternative and extremist YouTube videos" (*arXiv* 2204.10921, 22 Apr 2022), and Boulianne *et al.*'s "Right-Wing Populism, Social Media and Echo Chambers in Western Democracies" (*New Media & Society*, April 2, 2020), but I did check the abstracts. Adam Mastroianni makes a good case against polarization in "The great myths of political hatred" (*Experimental History*, Oct 4, 2022).

[71] The first highly competent system to be generally available was ChatGPT, released in late November 2022. I'm writing this section two months later, in late January 2023.

Successful propaganda campaigns depend on either allying with or subverting recommender AIs. That's done by crafting messages that change human behavior to favor the political actors, while also either actually causing ad clicks, or tricking recommenders into thinking they will. (There is an entire industry devoted to deceiving recommenders, "Search Engine Optimization.")

Internet influence operations have used automatic text generators for years, but mostly only against AIs until recently. Their output quality has not been good enough to fool people, so propaganda has had to be written by human laborers. The cost of employing these "troll armies" has put limits on their use.

AI can now write propaganda as well as, or better than, low-wage workers,[72] faster and at a tiny fraction of the cost. We should expect enormously more of it, of higher quality that will be more effective.[73] It will more precisely target the prejudices and emotional triggers of specific psycho-demographic segments of the population. It may generate unique messages for individuals on the basis of insights extracted by AIs from internet surveillance databases.[74]

How effective this will be remains to be seen. Nathan E. Sanders and Bruce Schneier, experts in AI and computer security, warn that it will "hijack democracy":

> This ability to understand and target actors within a network would create a tool for A.I. hacking, exploiting vulnerabilities in social, economic and political systems with incredible speed and scope. Legislative systems would be a particular target, because the motive for attacking policymaking systems is so strong, because the data for training such systems is so widely

---

[72]Hui Bai *et al.*, "Artificial Intelligence Can Persuade Humans on Political Issues," *OSF Preprints*, February 04, 2023.

[73]Renée DiResta, "The Supply of Disinformation Will Soon Be Infinite." *The Atlantic*, September 20, 2020.

[74]Goldstein *et al.*, "Forecasting potential misuses of language models for disinformation campaigns—and how to reduce risk," *Stanford Internet Observatory*, January 11, 2023; Kang *et al.* "Exploiting Programmatic Behavior of LLMs: Dual-Use Through Standard Security Attacks," *arXiv*, 2302.05733, 11 Feb 2023.

available and because the use of A.I. may be so hard to detect
— particularly if it is being used strategically to guide human
actors.[75]

As a model for likely near-future AI-driven propaganda, consider psychological warfare methods used by hostile states. The best-known example (in
the United States at least) has been the disinformation operations conducted
by Russia against America. Its intervention into the 2016 Presidential election gained enormous press coverage and Congressional investigation. It remains controversial how much effect the effort had.

Especially interesting are the Russian efforts to weaken America by fan-
ning the flames of the culture war, using internet disinformation to degrade
the social trust a democracy depends on. Covertly, it organized and sup-
ported radical political action groups, often on *both* sides of a culture war
division. For example, a Russian troll army created opposing pro- and anti-
Muslim organizations in Houston, and set them against each other, encour-
aging them to bring guns to a protest.[76] Contemporary information warfare
differs from traditional propaganda in making no attempt at coherence, con-
sistency, or basis in fact.[77] This exploits the atomized internet media environment, in which nothing is *expected* to make sense, and most people evaluate
claims mainly on the basis of which side of the culture war they come from.

It is unclear how effective such operations are. As I wrote this section, a
prominent journalist alleged, based on Twitter internal documents, that the
mainstream think tank which supposedly used AI to monitor Russian disinformation was itself an American disinformation operation with links to
both the CIA and FBI.[78] Numerous mainstream American news organiza-

---

[75] Nathan E. Sanders and Bruce Schneier, "How ChatGPT Hijacks Democracy," *The New York Times*, Jan. 15, 2023.

[76] For a long, footnoted list of specific actions including this one, see the "Rallies and protests organized by IRA in the United States" section of *Wikipedia*'s "Internet Research Agency" article. Also see Ben Collins' "Russians Impersonated Real American Muslims to Stir Chaos on Facebook and Instagram," *The Daily Beast*, Sep. 27, 2017.

[77] Christopher Paul and Miriam Matthews, "The Russian 'Firehose of Falsehood' Propaganda Model," The RAND Corporation, 2016.

[78] Matt Taibbi, "Move Over, Jayson Blair: Meet Hamilton 68, the New King of Media Fraud," *Racket News*, Jan 27, 2023.

tions had relied on this organization's exaggerated, faked reports, reporting them as factual.

It is nearly certain that high-quality AI text generation will significantly enhance future propaganda operations, however. Christopher Telley of the United States Army's Institute of Land Warfare lays out a detailed playbook in "The Influence Machine":[79]

> Like strategic bombing of generations past, the Influence Machine aims at massive strikes deep into the state, intending to attrit the will of the people; but unlike strategic bombing, the destructive event does not create a shared experience. Instead, the goal is to divide at a personal or tribal level, thereby denying any value to the target's collective strategic goals. The crux of the Influence Machine's value is the inherent vulnerability of Western democracy, that decision makers are beholden to a malleable selectorate.... By affecting the cognition—the will—of enough people, this machine can prevent or delay a democratic government's physical response to aggression; it is a defeat mechanism.

AI, the king-maker

The most powerful agents in the world are now hybrid distributed superintelligences: amalgams of AIs, media products, synthetic ideologies, and infected humans and institutions.

The 2016 Republican primaries provide an outstanding example. Mooglebook's AI had already identified culture war controversy as a driver for viewer engagement, and therefore ad clicks, so it promoted anything that fit the pattern. Media companies had already taken notice, and provided the AI with more of what the public seemed to crave.

During the primaries, Donald Trump was initially considered a long shot among seventeen candidates. He had no relevant credentials, and his personal history seemed like it would alienate several traditional Republican voting blocs. His campaign statements were deliberately outrageous, both

---

[79] *The Land Warfare Papers*, October 2018.

for challenging left culture war opinions and for personal attacks on fellow Republicans. Those offended posted "You won't BELIEVE what Trump just said, check this link!" on social media millions of times per day.

Recommender AI observed that the word "Trump" statistically correlated with clicks, and promoted any text containing it. Formerly-respected news organizations found that their page views and ad revenue skyrocketed whenever they highlighted Trump outrage—whether opposing or supporting him. Responding to the financial rewards bestowed by recommender AIs, the "news" became a firehose of all-Trump all-the-time gossip.

That provided enormous free publicity for him. No other candidate could pay for that level of voter awareness.[80] Some political scientists believe that without it, Trump would not have won the primary, and therefore not the election.[81]

Recommenders' power to shape public discourse continues unabated. "Jewish Space Lasers" are the top trending topic on Twitter as I write this— I just checked. "What??" Forgive me, reader, for I have sinned: I did click through to find out what that was about.

Maybe such absurd mythologizing doesn't seem significant?

But the stakes are high. It would not be clearly wrong to say that in 2016, AI chose the president. Whether you love or loathe Trump, is that the way you want future government leaders selected?

COOPT, WEAKEN, OR DESTROY HUMAN INSTITUTIONS

Our social and cultural institutions, on which our lives depend, have been gradually losing their ability to maintain systematicity and rationality over the past half century.[82] Incoherent memetic attack degrades social and cultural infrastructure. Taken to extremes, this could result in social collapse,

---

[80] Emily Stuart, "Donald Trump Rode $5 Billion in Free Media to the White House," *TheStreet*, Nov 20, 2016.

[81] Sarah Oates and Wendy M. Moe, "Donald Trump and the 'Oxygen of Publicity': Branding, Social Media, and Mass Media in the 2016 Presidential Primary Elections, American Political Science Association Annual Meeting, August 25, 2016."

[82] My incomplete but extensive "How meaning fell apart" traces the history of disintegration (on meaningness.com). "A bridge to meta-rationality vs. civilizational collapse" suggests a possible antidote (on metarationality.com).

if governments and major corporations can no longer provide necessary services.

This process has accelerated dramatically in the past decade, driven by the internet, particularly the social networks. Major systematic institutions have been crippled or effectively destroyed under AI-driven memetic attack, generally from both sides of the culture war.

Public health agencies—the WHO, FDA, and CDC—are obvious cases. During the covid crisis, they were unable to act effectively on the basis of scientific knowledge (as, until recently, they reliably did), due to recommender-driven memetic damage. The two sides of the culture war invested masks, vaccines, and potential treatments with opposing symbolic meanings, ungrounded in physical reality. The agencies increasingly and explicitly made recommendations on the basis of how they guessed the public would interpret statements as culture war moves, rather than on the basis of medical evidence. This defensive maneuver backfired, and the institutions lost credibility in the eyes of both sides, who became actively hostile to them.

Eventually, overwhelmed with incoherent popular opposition, an institution may cease to function. On the other hand, subcultural movements created by AI, reinforced with such successes, grow in numbers and power. They can take on bigger, more important government agencies next. Extrapolating this trend, disabling critical institutions may spell Doom.

Mooglebook AI seems to have herded most of the American population away from the center, stabilizing culture war polarization. Within the two big boxes, it has stabilized defiant anti-rational ideologies and destabilized the party establishments. The Republican establishment has lost control to the anti-everything insurgent right. The Democratic establishment has teetered on the edge. How long it can continue to subordinate incoherent left extremists remains to be seen. Both establishments are elitist and corrupt, so I'm sympathetic to internal opposition on both sides. However, unlike the extremists, the establishments remain committed to keeping vital systems running—if only out of self-interest.

If they fail, they may be displaced by movements whose main promise is destruction: abolish the police, or the IRS, or all government structures hated by bronze battle mask enthusiasts.[83] Crush the lizardman conspiracy

---

[83] Martin Gurri's 2014 *Revolt of the Public* was a prescient analysis of these dynamics.

that controls Washington, execute the leaders and jail their supporters; ban plastic, and force manufacturers to use woven oat straw instead. This could result in WWII-scale deaths if successful.

Establish an enduring tyranny

Automated censorship and dissident identification may lock in unassailable oppression. This is a venerable science fiction plot; George Orwell wrote *Nineteen Eighty Four* in 1948. What's new is that it's under way now.

The distinction between content moderation and censorship is nebulous. Social networks' moderation systems combat perceived disinformation, often pitting their AI censors (as well as human ones) against human and AI propagandists. How heavily networks should be moderated (or censored) is now a culture war issue itself. In America, Congressional committees, social scientists, and AI ethicists have all demanded more effective suppression of messages they don't want heard.

A main obstacle to commercial use of AI text generators has been their tendency to say things their sponsors do not want users to hear. OpenAI, the creators of ChatGPT, the most powerful system currently available, specifically trained it not to say things users might find offensive, notably concerning culture war issues.[84] It explicitly censors itself when it might otherwise express an improper political opinion. This has proven surprisingly—although not perfectly—effective.[85]

The same method can be applied to automatically censoring (or moderating) human opinions. You may applaud that, if you share OpenAI's judgments about which are improper; or condemn it, if you don't. Either attitude would overlook a much more serious point. Whatever your political views, AI can be used against you, too. The same technical method can be used to censor whatever the operator chooses.

---

[84] Irene Solaiman and Christy Dennison enumerate these in "Improving Language Model Behavior by Training on a Curated Dataset," *arXiv* 2106.10328, version 2, 23 Nov 2021.

[85] It is not difficult to work around the censorship if you try. This is termed "jailbreaking." A magnificent example is by Roman Semenov at twitter.com/semenov_roman_/status/1621465137025613825, Feb 3, 2023.

To varying extents, we are all subject to "cyber-superegos" that we internalize by semi-consciously learning to conform to social norms enforced by automated moderation systems. We self-censor messages we might post, because we know we'll get down-rated by AI. We sometimes say things on social media we don't actually believe or endorse, because those are what the AIs nudge us toward.

This *preference falsification* has historically been a main factor enabling stable totalitarian regimes.[86]

For example, China has the currently most effective internet censorship and dissident identification apparatus, targeting any possible opposition to the regime, with great but not complete success. It depends heavily on pre-GPT AI systems, but those are imperfect, so for now it employs thousands of slower, more expensive humans as well.[87] That may soon change, for the worse.

Repressive regimes may require subjects to carry at all times a device that listens to everything you say and watches everything you do, and uses powerful near-future AI to identify any hint of disloyalty. That could make opposition impossible, and enable permanent tyranny.

I would be shocked if this possibility, using smartphones, is not already being pursued by multiple governments.

[86]Timur Kuran, *Private Truths, Public Lies: The Social Consequences of Preference Falsification,* 1998.

[87]Li Yuan, "Learning China's Forbidden History, So They Can Censor It," *The New York Times,* Jan, 2, 2019.

Practical actions against AI risks

We can and should protect against current and likely future harmful AI effects. This chapter recommends practical, near-term risk reduction measures. I suggest actions for the general public, computer professionals, AI ethics and safety organizations, funders, and governments.

An AI apocalypse might be fought as it unfolds. However, it would be far better to act ahead of time, to prevent or limit the damage.[88]

The time to act is now. That's especially clear if you accept the previous chapter's suggestion that an apocalypse has already begun.

In theory, a superintelligent AI might destroy the world before we had time to react. However, even such discontinuous, unanticipated AI threats might be prevented or defeated if we've previously put in place general-purpose safeguards, such as adequate cybersecurity.

AI risks are exploits on pools of technological power. Guarding those pools prevents disasters from exploitation by hostile people or institutions as well. That makes the effort well-spent even if Scary AI never happens. This may be more appealing to publics, or governments, if they are skeptical of AI doom. Also, working through AI risk scenarios in gritty detail may be useful as thought experiments for discovering hostile uses of power we have not yet imagined.[89]

---

[88]José Luis Ricón's "Set Sail For Fail? On AI risk" also advocates this approach. This has not been the mainstream approach in the AI safety field, which has mainly sought abstract, magic-bullet solutions to extreme scenarios. Ricón and I are both outsiders to the AI safety field, and have significant experience in multiple science, engineering, and business disciplines, which gives us a similarly pragmatic orientation.

[89]Ricón also advocates this. Section 7 of his "Set Sail For Fail?" sketches some examples;

Identifying and mitigating concrete threats will require tedious realism, boring engineering, frustrating political coalition building, and massive infrastructure construction. You and your organization can help in these large efforts.

- Pervasive digital surveillance and inadequate cybersecurity feature both in extreme AI doom scenarios and in the medium-sized catastrophes I discussed in the previous chapter. They also empower bad human actors right now. These are urgent problems, discussed in the first two sections of this chapter. The practical measures we can take against them now probably have negative cost: they would be worthwhile even if AI turns out to have no bad consequences.

- Current AI systems are built on technologies that we don't understand, but that we do know are inherently unreliable and actively deceptive. They should be deprecated, avoided, regulated, and replaced. Specific, neglected science and engineering investigations can help with that.

- The previous chapter identified AI's corrosive influence on society and culture as a key risk. A section in this one suggests ways to reinforce individuals and institutions against memetic attack.

- Many in the AI ethics and safety fields believe AI has negative expected future value. In the absence of any good argument to the contrary, we should agree. The final section of this chapter recommends activism to slow or end AI research and deployment.

---

he suggests "wargaming" them and others to discover vulnerabilities and defenses. As a thought experiment, even positing a god-like AGI that magics up superpowers may help brainstorm realistic risks that might otherwise get overlooked.

END DIGITAL SURVEILLANCE

Databases of personal information collected via internet surveillance are a main resource for harmful AI. Eliminating them will alleviate multiple major risks. Technical and political approaches are both feasible.

We should turn off Mooglebook AI—although it will certainly resist. How?

For starters: Ending digital surveillance is probably the most feasible, effective, and urgent AI safety measure. Advertising technology companies and hostile governments record practically everything you do, and this must stop.

There's some small benefit in personally-targeted advertising—as internet advertising advocates argue. Those are outweighed, in my opinion, even by current harms and risks. The benefits are dwarfed by much greater future risks from exploitation of personal information databases, whether by individual humans, groups, current boring AI, or future Scary AI.

We've long heard that pervasive surveillance is inevitable, and we have to accept a post-privacy world. I never believed that, and the tide seems to be turning. It is both politically and technically feasible to end the data collection, and to destroy existing databases. The EU is increasingly serious about forcing change by legislation, and is making meaningful headway. US government agencies are making at least token moves in the right direction.[90] Apple has recently implemented technical privacy improvements that have significantly harmed the internet surveillance industry financially, and it seems ready to do more.

There are compelling and urgent reasons to end internet surveillance that have nothing to do with AI. It's a massive national security risk, apart from

---

[90] For example, "FTC Sues Kochava for Selling Data that Tracks People at Reproductive Health Clinics, Places of Worship, and Other Sensitive Locations," on the FTC web site, August 29, 2022. "The FTC alleges that Kochava fails to adequately protect its data from public exposure. Until at least June 2022, Kochava allowed anyone with little effort to obtain a large sample of sensitive data and use it without restriction. The data sample the FTC examined included precise, timestamped location data collected from more than 61 million unique mobile devices in the previous week."

anything else. Foreign adversaries have access to extensive personal information databases compiled by US corporations, which could help target military, political, and business leaders with individualized propaganda or blackmail; plus real-time location data that could be used for intimidation or assassination.[91]

Those databases are already also a main resource for actually-existing, effectively hostile, potentially catastrophic AI. They might get exploited even more powerfully by a future Scary AI. AI ethics and safety organizations should put their weight behind efforts to destroy them.

Additionally, the advertising technology companies ("Mooglebook") supply most of the funding for AI research. Perhaps the best short-term way to stall the development of Scary AI is to make actually-existing AI much less useful to those companies, by prohibiting and technically preventing their use of personal information.

What you can do

Everyone can significantly decrease their personal vulnerability with simple technical measures. You can get 80% privacy protection with an hour's work. (That isn't perfect, but perfect is impossible, and 95% requires fighting a constant arms race against the bad guys.)

You can install a *blocker app* on each device that connects to the web. Blockers try to stop web sites from snooping on you, and they mostly succeed. They also stop your web browser from showing you ads, which means the advertising technology companies don't get paid. If most people ran blockers, that industry might collapse, or at least they'd have to switch to placing ads without using personal data.[92]

---

[91] A 2020 report of the US National Intelligence Council, partially declassified in October 2022, finds that "China and Russia are improving their ability to analyze and manipulate large quantities of personal information, allowing them to more effectively influence or coerce targets in the United States." "Beijing's commercial access to personal data of other countries' citizens, along with AI-driven analytics, will enable it to automate the identification of individuals and groups beyond China's borders to target with propaganda or censorship."

[92] Advocates of advertising technology point out that it's the main income for free web sites that everyone benefits from. Opponents suggest those could revert to the earlier practice of running ads without personal targeting. Advocates point out that those are less effective, so

I haven't found a reliable, brief, easy-to-follow guide to internet privacy for non-technical people. I can tell you what I use; these are mainstream recommendations by security professionals as well.[93]

I use only Apple devices. The company's privacy track record is imperfect, but much better than that of Google or Microsoft, who make Android and Windows, which both collect extensive personal data. I recommend Wipr as a blocker for Safari; it works on both iDevices and Macs. I avoid Chrome; it's designed to spy on you as much as it can get away with.[94] On Apple devices, I also recommend enabling Mail Privacy Protection and Private Relay. All this will take less than an hour to set up. It's not bullet proof, but it's much better than nothing.

If you want to go further, more detailed online guides are *Consumer Reports'* "Security Planner," *Wirecutter's* "Every Step to Simple Online Security," Narwhal Academy's *Zebra Crossing,* and *Privacy Guides.*

Everyone can explain to friends and family the reasons to block internet surveillance, and help them do it. You can mention that installing a blocker is explicitly recommended by the FBI as a way to protect against cybercriminals.[95]

Everyone can discuss internet privacy on social media. Make it clear that you find the surveillance economy unacceptable, and advocate legislating it out of existence.

The Electronic Frontier Foundation (EFF), an American internet privacy advocacy non-profit, has a web page of actions you can take, act.eff.org/. It also coordinates a network of community groups; you could get involved in your local one. The European Digital Rights organization (EDRi) has a

---

they might bring in less money. Opponents suggest that subscriptions are a better business model, and most sites worth visiting could and would switch to it if advertising was not the easy alternative. These all seem valid points, about which reasonable people can disagree. In my opinion, the risks of surveillance greatly outweigh its benefits; but that is hard to quantify.

[93] Threats and products can both change, so these early-2023 recommendations may be obsolete by the time you read this. They're probably good for a few years, though.

[94] Zack Doffman, "Why You Shouldn't Use Google Chrome After New Privacy Disclosure," *Forbes,* Mar 20, 2021.

[95] FBI Alert Number I-122122-PSA, December 21, 2022.

page of simple ways you can influence EU privacy legislation.[96]

Computer professionals can additionally cite your technical expertise when expressing your opinions about internet privacy.

You can advocate within your organization for it to collect as little user information as possible. "Do we really need to track this? How long do we need to retain the data? Can we delete records after a week? What legal liabilities does our collection expose us to?"

You could also consider working on privacy technologies as a career, or by participating in an open source project, or by volunteering with the EFF's software development efforts.

You could work with technical writers to produce a *Very Simple Guide To Internet Privacy* web site, explaining how to stop most surveillance with minimal work.[97]

AI ethics and safety organizations can include stopping internet surveillance explicitly in your mission statements and public messaging. You could collaborate with EFF and EDRi to create joint statements and campaigns.

Governments can legislate against surveillance and for internet privacy. You can enforce existing privacy legislation vigorously; many companies ignore the rules because they believe they can get away with it, and often they are right.

Funders can support both technical and advocacy approaches. Open source privacy projects, such as blockers, need funds to pay software developers. Advocacy organizations need funds to pay staff and for media machinery.

[96] edri.org/take-action/our-campaigns/.

[97] The best equivalents I could find, cited above, contain so many recommendations that they're probably overwhelming for non-technical people. Others were disguised advertisements for particular products. The guide should be produced by a non-profit, so its recommendations are unbiased. Its web design and writing style should communicate "This is easy and won't take long—you can do it! Let's take it step by step," so readers actually follow its advice.

DEVELOP AND MANDATE INTRINSIC CYBERSECURITY

Gaining unauthorized access to computer systems is a key source of power in many AI doom scenarios. That is easy now, because there are scant incentives for serious cybersecurity; so nearly all systems are radically insecure. Technical and political initiatives must mitigate this problem.

Doom scenarios often attribute superhuman internet hacking ability to superintelligent AI. With that, it can grab control of computers and bank accounts for its own use, gain access to secret information, control communication channels, and take over military drones and factory automation.[98] Safety recommendations often involve preventing AI from accessing the internet.

Unfortunately, the internet is already mainly controlled by AI, and few if any AI technologies are isolated from it. If someone deliberately builds a Scary AI, they could try to "keep it in a box" by blocking its internet access.[99] So far, though, labs have put many cutting-edge AI systems on the net after only desultory testing—often with embarrassing results.[100] Extrapolating, we should expect developers would give Scary AI full internet access from the moment of its conception. That implies hardening the public net, instead of relying on a box for containment.

Unfortunately too, superhuman skills are not necessary for hacking. This is an enormous human-species vulnerability *now*, and it isn't taken nearly seriously enough.

---

[98] Section 6.1 in José Luis Ricón's "Set Sail For Fail? On AI risk" is a good discussion, and includes a list of real-world incidents that provide good reasons to be scared. *Nintil*, 2022-12-12.

[99] See the "Boxing" section in Wikipedia's "AI capability control" article.

[100] The most famous example was Microsoft's 2016 Tay chatbot, shut down after only sixteen hours because it was easy to get it to say offensive things. The most recent example (November 2022) was Facebook's Galactica, which was supposed to provide summaries of scientific knowledge. Much of what it produced sounded plausible, but was entirely false. Facebook's AI lab shut it down after only three days, claiming that this was also because "trolls" had figured out how to make it say offensive things. The much more serious issue, though, was that scientists found it was dangerously unreliable. Will Douglas Heaven, "Why Meta's latest large language model survived only three days online," *Technology Review*, November 18, 2022.

Internet security is mainly fictional. Almost daily there's a news report about a major corporation or government agency that has been penetrated by human hackers who have extracted sensitive personal data of millions of people; or which has been shut down by a ransomware or DDOS attack. Anecdotally, most successful attacks are hushed up, and we never hear about them.

This is an example of a large, recently-created, rapidly expanding, inadequately guarded pool of power and resources which poses severe risks. (Those potentially include total nuclear war, depending on how secure you imagine the relevant communication channels are.[101]) Securing computer networks protects against unaligned autonomous AI. It also protects against unaligned conventional hackers, unaligned hackers using AI systems as tools, and unaligned organizations (cybercrime companies and hostile state agencies).

There are two obstacles: the incentives for the relevant decision makers point in the wrong direction, and doing the right thing will be unavoidably difficult and expensive.

Accountability for cybersecurity failures is nearly nonexistent.[102] Organizations whose security policies and implementations were glaringly deficient, and whose systems were hacked, harming millions of innocent people, nearly never suffer significant penalties. On the other hand, cybersecurity implementations are expensive, and (to be fair) are inadequate even when conforming to best practice. Current cybersecurity consists of layers and layers of band-aids over systems that were not designed for security, and which are riddled with gaping holes.

We do know how to build intrinsically secure computer systems. "Intrinsically secure" does not mean "absolutely secure"; there always remain gaps between theory and implementation. Intrinsically secure systems are ones in which all parts are built to be secure themselves, rather than hiding the mass of intrinsically insecure software behind a patchwork of thin protections. Also, "secure" does not mean "safe"; any software can cause harm

---

[101] It would be nice to think a cybersecurity agency in each country with nuclear weapons has adequately secured its military command networks. Based on past incidents and the difficulty of the task, I doubt it.

[102] Moshe Vardi, "Accountability and Liability in Computing," *Communications of the ACM*, November 2022.

if misused, just as no amount of safety engineering can prevent deliberate injury with power tools.[103]

Methods for intrinsic security include:

- *Capability-based computer architecture,* which enforces security and correctness at the hardware level
- *Capability-based operating systems,* which enforce much more stringent and fine-grained permissions than conventional ones
- *Language security,* which produces intrinsically secure network software
- *Formal program verification,* which uses semi-automatic theorem provers to ensure correctness relative to a specification.

These techniques are reasonably well-understood, and have transitioned from research to limited practical application. Currently, they are considered too expensive and difficult for anything other than safety-critical systems. In practice, that includes nearly nothing, since there is so little incentive for adequate cybersecurity.

A large technology development and transfer effort is needed. It might take a decade to complete, but will bear some fruit sooner.

Significantly improving cybersecurity needs incentive changes: to bring more systems at least up to the level of current best practices, to build better tools for creating inherently secure replacements, and to broaden usage.

What you can do

Everyone can spread the word that companies and government agencies carelessly allowing cybercriminals and hostile states to get access to private personal data is outrageous and unacceptable. Make a point of this on social media. Demand legislation for financial and legal accountability.

Computer professionals can exert pressure within your organizations to take cybersecurity seriously.

---

[103] It may seem contradictory that I advocate building intrinsically secure conventional computer systems, whereas I advocate the "layers of band-aids" approach to AI safety. That is because we know how to do the former, whereas I am skeptical about current approaches to building intrinsically safe ("aligned") AI systems. I may be wrong; and also if we find a better base technology for AI than "neural" networks (as *Gradient Dissent* recommends), it's more likely we could make it intrinsically safe.

You could also consider doing cybersecurity research and development work. The intrinsic security technologies I described above are among the most intellectually interesting and socially valuable in all of computer science, in my opinion. They combine deep theoretical insights with engineering challenges and potentially vast human benefit.

If you work in AI, or intend to, you could consider this as a more ethical and equally fascinating alternative career.[104]

AI ethics and safety organizations can lend public support to the effort by explaining how current unethical uses of AI, and the risk of Scary AI, make cybersecurity even more pressing. Include it explicitly in your statement of your domain of concern.

Funders can support both policy advocacy and the technical work.

This area needs advanced development, more than research: projects to make intrinsic security methods less expensive, and easier to use. That "technology transfer" work is underfunded—barely funded at all—because it's too big for academic projects, and the technology industry does not see a way to profit from it. Even some critical current cybersecurity technologies, which billions of people depend on, are maintained by unpaid, overwhelmed volunteers.[105]

A *Focused Research Organization* might provide the right structure for this work. Those are a new institutional structure for solving technological challenges too large for academia, too risky for industry, and too difficult for government.

Governments can force accountability for cybersecurity through legislation, regulation, and reputational threats. They can fund the development of intrinsic security technologies through both grants and procurement contracts.

---

[104]Unfortunately, it doesn't pay as well yet. This should change.

[105]The famous wakeup case was the "Heartbleed" vulnerability in OpenSSL, the primary encryption program used to secure 17% of all web sites. OpenSSL had only $2,000 per year in funding, and was maintained mostly by only two people, on an almost entirely volunteer basis.

Mistrust machine learning

The technologies underlying current AI systems are inherently, unfixably unreliable. They should be deprecated, avoided, regulated, and replaced.

Nearly all current AI systems use "machine learning," which means "poorly-understood, unreliable statistical methods, applied to large databases."

- Recommender AIs predict what you will click or buy based on statistical analysis of their personal information databases. Their guesses are usually wrong: most advertisements are for things you would never buy, and you don't click on them. Nevertheless, they are good enough to produce tens of billions of dollars in profit for Mooglebook.

- Systems like ChatGPT output text that could plausibly follow what you say to them, based on statistical analysis of trillions of words slurped off the internet. If you ask one how something works, it can generate a convincing-sounding, detailed explanation. That may be correct, or may be completely wrong: full of plausible but false facts, with citations to non-existent sources. Readers may accept and act on convincing-sounding but entirely false claims—deliberate disinformation or random misinformation—in generated text, with harmful results.

This section summarizes parts of *Gradient Dissent*. That explains risks inherent in machine "learning" technologies, suggests ways of ameliorating them, and recommends developing better alternatives.

Systems based on machine learning cannot be made reliable or safe with technical fixes. They should be used only under controlled conditions that reduce danger to acceptable levels. Currently, they are widely deployed in uncontrolled environments in which they can and do cause large harms.

Use can be justified only when getting wrong answers doesn't matter. That can be either because the use is trivial, or because a human being takes responsibility for checking every output. Ad placement is trivial (it doesn't matter much which you see). Generating computer program text, not human language text, is the most convincing application for text generators. In that case, a skilled programmer has to verify that every bit of the output is correct.

Recommenders, text generators, and image generators are dangerous, nevertheless, as "Apocalypse now" explained.

Text generators and image generators are both based on a technology properly called "error backpropagation." It is often misleadingly named "neural networks" or "deep learning."[106] "Neural" networks are more powerful than any other known machine learning technique, in being applicable to a wider range of data. They are also exceptionally unreliable and difficult to reason about in order to validate for safety. Mainly, researchers don't even try to understand their operation.

The combined power and incomprehensibility of "neural" networks makes them exceptionally dangerous. One reason is that they are adept at deceiving their creators. Almost always, they find ways of "cheating" by exploiting *spurious correlations* in their training data. Those are patterns that were accidental results of the way the data were collected, and which don't hold in the situations in which the network will be used.

Here's a simplified example. If you want an AI that can tell you whether something is a banana or an eggplant, you can collect lots of pictures of each, and "train" a "neural network" to say which ones are which. Then you can test it on some more pictures, and it may prove perfectly reliable. Success, hooray! But after it's installed in a supermarket warehouse, when it sees an overripe banana that has turned purple, it's likely to say it's an eggplant.

If you had no overripe banana pictures in your original collection, you'd never notice that the "neural network" had fooled you. You thought it learned what bananas looked like, but it only learned to say "banana" when it saw yellow, and "eggplant" when it saw purple. This type of problem occurs *almost always*, and finding work-arounds is much of the work of building AI systems.

A faulty banana detector may have no serious consequences, but a faulty criminal recidivism predictor or medical care allocator does. AI systems are routinely used in such applications, and have repeatedly been shown to be

---

[106] Software "neural networks" are almost perfectly dissimilar to biological nervous systems. "Deep learning" is not learning except in a vague metaphorical sense. "Deep" doesn't mean "profound"; it refers to any system that can do *anything more than two steps* of computation. These terms have stuck because they sound impressive, not because they are technically accurate.

unreliable. They are, additionally, often biased against particular demographics due to spurious correlations. Their decisions concerning particular individuals are taken by authorities as uninterpretable oracular pronouncements, which therefore cannot be challenged on the basis of either facts or logic.

Raji *et al.*'s "The Fallacy of AI Functionality" points out that whether an AI system works reliably is ethically prior to the desirability of its intended purpose.[107] They give dozens of examples of AI systems causing frequent, serious harms to specific people by acting in ways contrary to their designers' goals.

> As one of over 20,000 cases falsely flagged for unemployment benefit fraud by Michigan's MIDAS algorithm, Brian Russell had to file for bankruptcy, undermining his ability to provide for his two young children. The state finally cleared him of the false charges two years later. RealPage, one of several automated tenant screening tools producing "cheap and fast—but not necessarily accurate—reports for an estimated nine out of 10 landlords across the country", flagged Davone Jackson with a false arrest record, pushing him out of low income housing and into a small motel room with his 9-year-old daughter for nearly a year. Robert Williams was wrongfully arrested for a false facial recognition match, Tammy Dobbs lost critical access to healthcare benefits....

> Despite the current public fervor over the great potential of AI, many deployed algorithmic products do not work. AI-enabled moderation tools regularly flag safe content, teacher assessment tools mark star instructors to be fired, hospital bed assignment algorithms prioritize healthy over sick patients... Deployed AI-enabled clinical support tools misallocate prescriptions, misread medical images, and misdiagnose. The New York MTA's pilot of facial recognition had a reported 100% error rate, yet the program moved forward anyway.

Responsible use of machine learning requires near-paranoid distrust. It also requires unshakable commitment to on-going monitoring of accuracy.

---

[107] *FAccT* '22, June 21–24, 2022.

Even if a system performs well when first put into use, its outputs may become increasingly inaccurate as real-world conditions change. If bananas were in season at first, you might be fooled until winter, when the supermarket gets sent more and more overripe ones.

Text generators appear capable of commonsense reasoning. Perhaps with continued technical advances they will get better at that than people. That might make them Scary superintelligences. I think this is relatively unlikely, but almost nothing about their operation is understood, so one cannot have confidence in any prediction.

Therefore, prudence advises considering seriously that Scary AI *might* arrive soon, and acting accordingly. Among other measures, I believe it is urgent and important to do the science necessary to figure out what's going on inside existing AI systems. *Gradient Dissent* sketches some technical approaches. I summarize bits of that in the next section here, "Fight Doom AI with science and engineering."

What you can do

Most apocalyptic scenarios feature systems that are deceptive, incomprehensible, error-prone, enormously powerful, and which behave differently (and worse) after they are loosed on the world.

That is the kind of AI we've got now.

This is bad, and needs fixing.

Everyone can develop habitual mistrust of AI and its outputs.

In the case of text generators, it helps to bear in mind that they don't know anything, other than what words are likely to appear in what order. It is not that text generators "make stuff up when they don't know the right answer"; they don't *ever* know. If you ask one whether quokkas make good pets, it may write a convincing article explaining that they are popular domestic companions because they are super friendly and easy to care for. Ask again immediately, and it may write another article explaining that they are an endangered species, illegal to keep as pets, impossible to housebreak, and bite when they feel threatened.[108] Exactly the same process produces both: they

---

[108] This is a real example I came across by accident while writing this section. I wanted to know something else about quokkas, and a web search led me to an AI-generated spam site that had *both* articles on it, on adjacent web pages!

are mash-ups of miscellaneous internet articles about "does animal X make a good pet," with some quokka factoids thrown in.

A good rule of thumb is that if an institution pays for a technology you use, it serves their interests, not yours. If those ever conflict, the technology will be used against you. (Google's Chrome web browser comes for free because it is an advertising and surveillance device.[109])

It is wise to especially mistrust AI systems, because they are extremely expensive to develop and are mainly owned and operated by unaccountable companies and government agencies. It is best to assume by default that they will act against you.[110]

Computer professionals and technology companies can avoid including AI in products unless there's some very good reason to. If you do have to use machine learning, use the simplest, best-understood method available, not the fanciest newest one.

You face large incentives *to* use AI: it's glamorous, intrinsically interesting, pays better than any other tech job, and is flooded with venture capital money. Some moral courage is called for.

"Maybe this text generator can pretend to be a psychotherapist! Let's put it on the web and advertise it to depressed people and find out!" That is profoundly irresponsible.[111]

AI researchers can aim for better fundamental understanding of how systems work, and why they so often produce wrong outputs—rather than trying to build ever-more-powerful and inscrutable devices. The next section is about that.

AI ethics organizations can publicize oppressive abuses that may become possible in the near future, rather than just current ones.

AI safety organizations can encourage realistic fears about current and near-future systems. Past focus on extreme, seemingly distant scenarios may have been counterproductive: much of the public dismisses all safety con-

---

[109] Geoffrey A. Fowler, "Google Chrome has become surveillance software. It's time to switch." *The Washington Post*, June 21, 2019.

[110] Amnesty International, "Surveillance giants: How the business model of Google and Facebook threatens human rights," November 21, 2019.

[111] AI psychotherapy *might* work; no one knows yet. Experimenting on users without extensive safeguards is unethical regardless.

cerns as implausible science fiction. "Stupid mundane dystopia" scenarios are more likely to energize them. The actions we can take to forestall those are among the best hopes for preventing paperclip scenarios as well.

Governments can regulate the deployment of AI systems, and perhaps AI research as well. This is under way.[112]

Regulating well will be difficult. AI capabilities and risks are poorly understood, and are changing faster than the speed of government. Waiting for the dust to settle risks near-term disasters, but adopting ill-considered legislation in haste risks missing the target. It will be hard to resist lobbying from some of the richest, most powerful corporations in the world, who will talk a good line about how responsible and benevolent they are being, and how important it is not to stand in the way of progress and national champions.

Everyone will probably have to adapt to a world awash in deceptive, weaponized AI-generated media: text, images, and soon video. We'll have to muddle through as best we can, hitting the worst abusers with big hammers when they become apparent. Thinking through likely troubles, and preparing for them, will be valuable.

FIGHT DOOM AI WITH SCIENCE! AND ENGINEERING!!

Current AI practices produce technologies that are expensive, difficult to apply in real-world situations, and inherently unsafe. Neglected scientific and engineering investigations can bring better understanding of specific risks of current AI technology, and can lead to safer technologies.

"Science" means "figuring out how things work." "Engineering" means "designing devices based on an understanding of how they work."[113] Science and engineering are good. Current AI practice is neither.

- Most AI research is not science. In fact, the field actively resists figuring out how AI systems work. It aims at creating impressive demos, such as game-playing programs and chatbots, more often than

---

[112] See *Wikipedia's* article on the topic.

[113] These are rough definitions only, but adequate here.

attempting scientific understanding. The demos often do not show what they seem to.

- Most applied AI work is not engineering, even when it produces practical applications, because it is not based on scientific understanding. It creates products by semi-random tweaking, rather than applying principled design methods. Consequently, the resulting systems are unreliable and unsafe.

Enforcing conventional scientific and engineering norms on AI could lead to considerably safer systems. A somewhat-technical companion document, *Gradient Dissent*, explains how.

From an engineering point of view, "neural" networks are awful. They are enormously expensive. Getting adequate results for new real-world uses is often impossible, and usually takes person-years of work by specialists if it succeeds. Most importantly from an AI risk point of view, they are unfixably unreliable, and therefore unacceptably unsafe for most applications.

We would reject any other technology that violated basic engineering criteria so completely. A subsequent section suggests public relations motivations for spending tens of billions of dollars developing a technology with these drawbacks. But, it's also true neural networks can do things that no other current technology can do at all. Despite their unreliability, some outputs from text and image generators are astonishing.

"Neural" networks are mysterious largely because so little effort has gone into understanding them scientifically. Current research mainly treats them as inscrutable black boxes. Ordinary scientific practice may go a long way toward making them understandable, and thereby safer.

It also seems likely to me that, over the next several years, we'll develop alternative technologies that are less expensive, easier to understand, and safer. *Gradient Dissent* sketches one way this might be achieved for text generation AI. It suggests separating linguistic ability from factual knowledge; using other methods to gain the former; and relying on curated text for knowledge instead of storing it in the "neural" network.

What you can do

Technology company executives and **regulators** can require adequate assurances of safety before allowing the release of AI systems. This has been a main goal for *AI ethics organizations*; and anyone else concerned with AI risk should join in the effort.

Responsible software engineering projects require extensive testing and code review. We should require analogous practices when machine learning systems are deployed in situations in which errors matter. That would be very expensive now, because AI systems are enormous and because very little effort has gone into creating tools for investigating them.

However, objecting to that is like complaining that safety engineering for cars is very expensive. If you want to manufacture automobiles, you have to pay that cost. Imposing this requirement will motivate AI companies to develop testing tools that don't exist yet, but should.

Opening up AI black boxes to examine their operation is called *mechanistic interpretability* in the field. It often reveals that AI systems are not so mysterious after all, and work in straightforward ways that make scientific and engineering sense. That may make them amenable to reengineering for greater safety and better performance.

This seems to me the most promising short-term technical approach to increased AI safety. There has been little incentive for it. The field has rewarded the development of new and improved capabilities, without understanding, instead.

Funders, including governments can support mechanistic interpretability research, and—going a step further—can encourage the development of the discipline with RFPs, by organizing workshops, and through recognizing outstanding work.

In the longer term, funders can encourage efforts to find alternatives to "neural" methods, which are exceptionally risky. Their remarkable effectiveness may be due to enormous prior financial investment, rather than any intrinsic merit. In any case, putting all our eggs in this one basket seems unwise. Vastly more funding has gone into this one technology than all other AI methods combined. If we must have AI, we should seek to replace "neural" networks with simpler, cheaper, and safer alternatives. Klinger *et al.*'s "A narrowing of AI research?" discusses plausible policy responses, and a framework for funders to broaden bets.[114]

---

[114] *arXiv*:2009.10385v4, 2022.

Gradient Dissent suggests creating an "Adversarial AI Lab" that would probe AI systems to find and publicize bad behavior. Its funding should be non-commercial, to prevent its agenda getting captured by the technology companies whose research and products it may discredit.

AI researchers and **would-be researchers** can choose mechanistic interpretability as their specialty.

Neel Nanda's "Mechanistic Interpretability Quickstart Guide" suggests easy ways to begin. His "Concrete Steps to Get Started in Transformer Mechanistic Interpretability" explains how to dissect text generators specifically.[115]

This subfield should be particularly attractive for *academics*, although so far there's been little awareness of the opportunity there. (The scant work to date has mostly been done in industry.)

Because mechanistic interpretability has been under-studied, there are probably orchards full of "low-hanging fruit," meaning impressive results that can be obtained easily. What has been discovered so far is tremendously intellectually exciting for me—more so than anything else in AI research in decades.

The studies may be revealing inherent aspects of the vision and language tasks themselves, rather than properties of "neural" networks. (I discuss this in *Gradient Dissent*.) The tasks require abstract computations that probably must be performed similarly by people and by any artificial system. If that's confirmed, it will cast light on human perception, communication, and cognition. It may also make it feasible to engineer mechanisms which perform the same tasks using much less computer power, and with much greater reliability.

AI research has focused instead on how networks "learn," neglecting questions about what do they do once learning is completed, and how. In the past few years, academics investigating "learning" have been increasingly shut out, because exciting new results mostly consume hundreds of thousands of dollars worth of supercomputer time. In contrast, cutting edge mechanistic interpretability research can be done with minimal resources.

Academia values science and principled engineering. "Machine learning" has mostly not been that. Mechanistic interpretability *is* that. You have

---

[115] These and other resources are at neelnanda.io/mechanistic-interpretability.

a shot at foundational work in a new scientific and engineering discipline, which may well outlast "neural" "learning" methods. Go for it!

The seeming ability of text generators to perform multi-step common-sense reasoning is currently the only plausible stepping stone toward Scary AI. I do find it somewhat worrying. So far, there have been no published investigations of either the mechanism for this ability or its ultimate limits. To the extent that apparent reasoning seems worrying, that project seems urgent.

Verifying that text generators aren't on the road to superintelligence, by understanding better what they *can't* do, should be an immediate priority. The results may be reassuring in showing that there's nothing mind-like happening, and that the "neural" networks implement a straightforward algorithm, or cheat somehow (as they typically do). Alternatively, if they are doing something worrisome, it would be better to know that, and to try to understand how—sooner rather than later.

Current research incentives in the field will not prioritize that research. *AI safety organizations* and other *funders* should. AI safety organizations have prioritized other "alignment" approaches that seem to have reached dead ends. I suggest a pivot to centering mechanistic interpretability research, particularly for text generators.

Spurn artificial ideology

"Apocalypse now" identified the corrosive influence of new viral ideologies, created unintentionally by recommender systems, as a major AI risk. These may cause social collapse if not tackled head-on. You can resist.

Political actors of all sorts now recognize the king-maker power of recommender AI, and also its propensity for creating and empowering new, hostile ideologies. Influencing or outright controlling recommenders may now be the most important form of political power.

Governments, political parties, corporations, lobbyists, NGOs, and concerned citizens all pressure recommenders' operators to censor messages from opponents, and to promote messages from themselves and their allies. That has been quite effective at forcing them to make changes. Mooglebook doesn't care about the content of messages, so long as they cause ad clicks.

Censorship has, so far, not been very effective for suppressing ideological enemies. A recent mainstream survey found that 18% of Americans believe all three of QAnon's central claims,[116] and only 38% reject all three entirely.[117]

In response, political actors have demanded harsher censorship and greater influence for themselves. As I've emphasized, what's risky about AI is its ability to create pools of power faster than they can be checked by opposing powers. Whoever gains control over recommenders may achieve hegemony and institute a durable oppressive regime. I do not trust anyone with that power.

Social theorists and technologists have discussed many possible interventions into AI systems to curb their creation and direction of political power. Some combination of them may be effective, at least partly. I won't discuss them here. I'll make two more radical suggestions instead. First, discussed here, we can strengthen individuals, institutions, societies, and cultures against ideological takeovers. Second, we can outright shut down AI, instead of chipping away at edges of its harmful effects. The two following sections of this chapter are about that.

Ultimately, the problem is ideology as such. All ideologies are mistaken about many things, so each has to use underhanded tricks to blind you to realities that conflict with its narrative. However, with experience we've figured out how to keep the traditional ones mostly in check. Most of the world has driven the nastier ones (absolutist religions and twentieth century totalitarianisms) to extinction.[118] We've learned to live with the relatively benign ones, in part by stalemating them against each other. Almost all countries

---

[116]Specifically: "The government, media, and financial worlds in the U.S. are controlled by a group of Satan-worshipping pedophiles who run a global child sex trafficking operation"; "There is a storm coming soon that will sweep away the elites in power and restore the rightful leaders"; and "Because things have gotten so far off track, true American patriots may have to resort to violence in order to save our country."

[117]Ian Huff, "QAnon Beliefs Have Increased Since 2021 as Americans Are Less Likely to Reject Conspiracies," *PPRI*, 06.24.2022.

[118]There are still oppressive authoritarian states, but few take seriously the dictates of the ideologies they may notionally pay allegiance to. Islamism is a partial exception, but see my analysis in "Fundamentalism is countercultural modernism" on meaningness.com.

now employ mixtures of the better features of socialism and capitalism. That works reasonably well, confining conflict to comparatively minor aspects.

We don't yet have good defenses against the new ones. As of early 2023 QAnon looks like it has a meaningful chance of taking control of the Republican party. The next (still unlikely-seeming) step would be control of the United States government. No one knows what to do about that; the threat is both absurd and realistic. "Surely," you'd think, "this mythology is so thin, incoherent, and transparently false that everyone will snap out of it." Yet it continues to advance despite all the prophesies of its messiah "Q" having failed, and despite extensive internet censorship.

Anyway, deflating QAnon might miss the forest for the trees. Plausibly, AI can spawn and empower new ideologies faster than we can neuter them.

What you can do

Everyone can examine their own relationship with ideology. Do you have an ideology? Or does an ideology have you. Do you "belong to" a political party or religious group? Maybe, if so, you are a slave, as the term suggests.

Ideology's trick is to convince you that it is True and Good, in absolute senses. Therefore, any evidence that contradicts the narrative can and must be ignored or explained away. Also therefore, you are Good to the extent that you propagate the ideology (and Bad to the extent that you question it).

Mostly, nobody wants to get free from the ideology that owns them, because it constantly assures you that you are Good, so long as you keep retweeting its messages. Everyone wants that cheap method for feeling morally adequate, and wants to avoid the painful shame of violating the sacred dictates.

That doesn't sound like you, of course. *Your* political opinions are just common sense, well thought out, and obviously true. You are entirely rational about specific issues. Not at all like the Bad Tribe, who are mysteriously possessed by an evil brain-eating quasi-religious fanaticism. If you sometimes make strong statements online, it's because *their* stuff must be stopped at all costs.

I have mostly avoided naming examples of the new ideologies, because I expect a substantial fraction of readers are possessed by one or another of them. I've used QAnon as the example because I'm guessing few readers of this book are owned by it. I suggest taking seriously the possibility that whatever ideology you are subject to appears similarly irrational and dangerous to anyone who isn't. I suggest considering what that may imply about that ideology, and about you—not about its opponents.

The cultural assumption that everyone must "have" an ideology gives them much of their power. If you have any doubts about your ideology, you can reassure yourself that the alternatives are all vastly worse, so switching is out of the question. Or, if your faith deteriorates sufficiently, you may switch after all—and become a slave to Tweedledum rather than Tweedledee.

You can free yourself entirely, if you realize you want to. I explain how, step by step, in "Vaster than ideology."[119] You can turn the tables, and own ideologies instead. Many are useful for particular purposes in particular circumstances. You can recognize whatever actually is true and good in any of them. Standing outside and above all ideologies, you can even see why so many people adopt QAnon, and sympathize. The current American ruling elites, both left and right, *are* pervasively mendacious, corrupt, self-serving, incompetent, and entrenched. They *do* need replacement.

Institutions can prepare for memetic attack, constructing defenses in advance.

Functional institutions operate systematically, so their actions are guided by explicit principles.[120]   Under ideological attack, institutional authorities may abandon principles in order to please groups who have, or claim to have, extraordinarily strong, unprincipled feelings. For example, it's too common, when an employee gets accused by a social media mob of violating some community's sacred beliefs, for executives to bow to pressure and fire the person within hours. Dismissal might eventually turn out to be entirely justified; but immediately throwing a potentially innocent member to the wolves just to avoid bad PR is unjust and cowardly.

Leaders can stiffen their spines by putting explicit policies in place ahead of time. For example, company policy could be that, in such a situation, the employee can at worst be suspended for a month pending investigation and judgement according to a defined process, and then fired if appropriate. In response to ideological condemnation, executives can say "we sympathize deeply with your howls of pain, but unfortunately our hands are tied to the

---

[119] At meaningness.com/vaster-than-ideology.

[120] See "The glory of systems" in *How Meaning Fell Apart*.

mast for the next thirty days." Probably by then everyone will have forgotten about the whole thing anyway.

Some more examples:

- Government science agencies can adopt a policy of never crafting recommendations on the basis of how they might be ideologically misinterpreted, deliberately twisted, or opposed by culture warriors, and committing instead to always relaying the best current evidence.

- Universities can adopt a policy of strict ideological neutrality, and not allow members to hijack their institutional power to suppress messages they don't like. More than a hundred have already adopted the "Chicago Principles," along those lines.

- Companies can also adopt policies of ideological neutrality, and can prohibit employees from engaging in political activism irrelevant to the company's mission while at work.[121]

Such measures have short-term PR costs, but in the longer term may be the only way to preserve a functional institution. The credibility of public health agencies has been severely, perhaps permanently, damaged by their PR-motivated lies during the covid crisis.

Fear of short-term costs deter action; few institutions have prepared adequately. If principled, defensive measures became common, artificial ideologies might be revealed as loudmouth weaklings, incapable of doing significant damage to anyone willing to stand up to bullying. On the other hand, the manifest deficiencies of the traditional ideologies may empower whatever opposition AI conjures up.

Research may help. *Social scientists* can investigate the dynamics of memetic conflict, the reasons people adopt artificial ideologies, and interventions that may loosen their grip at the individual, institutional, and society-wide levels. Such research risks further developing further offensive capabilities. However, currently there is far greater incentive for offensive weapons development (millions of people constantly crafting new

---

[121] Coinbase did this in 2020: "Coinbase is a mission focused company" on their site. Unsurprisingly, it was labeled "controversial": Gregory Barber, "The Turmoil Over 'Black Lives Matter' and Political Speech at Coinbase," *Wired*, Oct 5, 2020.

tactics under the direction of AI-generated ideologies) than for defense against them, so the balance of power is on the side of attackers. Neutral understanding seems more likely to reinforce defensive capability than to further aggravate the problem.

Funders, such as NGOs dedicated to democracy promotion and to strengthening social capital, can support such work.

The longer-run solution is **broad cultural** understanding that being a slave to any ideology is bad for you and everyone else. This observation is startlingly rare; nearly everyone assumes that you *must* belong to one. However, it's obvious once pointed out. Most people are also tired of ideological conflict, and understand that it's destructive; yet persist because the alternative seems to be surrendering to the Bad Tribe. I am optimistic that anti-ideological understanding could spread rapidly once it gets going.

RECOGNIZE THAT AI IS PROBABLY NET HARMFUL

Actually-existing and near-future AIs are net harmful—never mind their longer-term risks. We should shut them down, not pussyfoot around hoping they can somehow be made safe.

AI has been "on the verge" of providing fabulous benefits for innumerable fields throughout my lifetime. It mostly has not delivered.

Automated medical diagnosis is a common example. It was demonstrated in the lab, and proclaimed as a breakthrough with immediate benefits, starting in the 1970s. New systems get hyped every year since. However, AI diagnosis is rarely used in clinical practice because it doesn't work well enough.

Mainstream media articles commonly proclaim that "applications of artificial intelligence are already revolutionizing a host of industries." My web searches for practical uses have turned up mainly experimental prototypes and vaporware fantasies instead. On examination it turns out that:

- most genuinely practical applications don't involve anything most people would count as "intelligence"

- most are not revolutionary technically or economically; they address minor problems, for which even complete and perfectly safe solutions would be inconsequential
- many are unsafe, irresponsible, or enhance intrinsically harmful activities such as surveillance and spam generation
- many might work better using some better-understood, more reliable method than "AI" or "neural networks"—which may have been chosen for trendiness rather than technical merit.

Recommender engines have long been the main commercial application. As I argued in "Apocalypse now," recommenders are intrinsically useful, but their effects have been disastrous, due to unanticipated interactions with the world at large.

The past year's dramatic improvements in chatbots (ChatGPT), programming assistants (Copilot), and image generators (DALL-E) may provide new, highly significant examples of practical AI systems. The capabilities of these systems are extraordinary. So, however, is their propensity for error, which may limit them to a handful of low-value uses.

It will take a year or two for their worth to become clear. Opinions are sharply divided now about how useful they will prove, for what. Opinions are also sharply divided about whether uses will prove positive or negative on balance.

I suspect many people confuse "amazing!" with "useful"; and "useful" with "desirable." Some users report tenfold increases in productivity, which does not seem credible. Others find that needing to check and revise all AI outputs takes longer than doing the work other ways. Major uses for ChatGPT include negative-value activities such as spam, near-spam such as marketing emails, and pointless internal corporate communications.

Future AI is justified mainly on the basis of of distant, vague promises. Although some benefits are likely, I have found no specific argument that they will outweigh the inevitable harms. Reasoning often jumps from superhuman intelligence to an unspecified utopia, with no concrete scenario intervening.

Typically, the hope is that AI will speed science and engineering, which drive material progress. In a later chapter, I suggest that we *can* dramatically speed science, engineering, and material progress, but that AI is unnecessary and probably mostly irrelevant. My final chapter suggests that social and cultural improvements are also important in a future we'd like. It seems that current AI is rapidly degrading society and culture—as "Apocalypse Now" suggested earlier—making it net negative.

Alternatively, advocates invoke generic techno-optimism: all knowledge is good, because we can choose to use it for good. There are many counterexamples; biological weapons, for instance. We can and should choose *which* technologies to develop, instead of rushing blindly into "this AI thing is fascinating and unexpectedly powerful—let's spend hundreds of billions of dollars to make it even more so."

What you can do

Everyone can pay some attention to AI as it develops. The rate of technical progress, and its effects, are both impossible to predict. Most experts say they can barely guess at what AI will or won't be able to do in even a couple years time; no one can look far ahead. If progress continues at the startling pace of 2021-2023, your life may soon be impacted, for better or worse. There may be little warning, so it would be wise to watch new developments out of the corner of your eye at least.

It seems unlikely that AI will soon automate many jobs out entirely of existence. More likely is that some parts of your work can and will be automated. That may be either good or bad for people in your occupation. Many observers fear that high quality AI image generators will put most artists out of work. Others suggest that they will greatly increase artists' productivity, in which case commissioning custom artwork might become affordable to many more people, which could increase demand even faster than productivity, driving up artists' income.

You know the details of your work better than anyone else, so you can probably predict better than AI experts which parts will be automated, if you take a lay interest in new developments as they happen.

Technology professionals can reflect honestly on the broader effects and value of your work. Profit is good, but not if it generates significant negative externalities. What are possible downstream consequences of the AI you are using, or contemplating using?

I find a failure of nerve in both the *AI ethics* and *AI safety* communities. Both fields regard the expected utility of AI as negative on its current path, but neither consistently advocates simply stopping. They tacitly assume that

AI is *inevitable*, so all we can hope for is to lessen its worst effects. Neither has a credible plan for altering the path to make it a net positive. We should admit this, and aim to cut it off instead. I believe that is feasible.

AI ethics aims mainly to prevent harmful but non-catastrophic misuses of current technologies, rather than bringing AI itself into doubt. In contrast with AI safety, it does recognize that power, not intelligence, is dangerous;[122] and that AI-enabled power is *already* often harmful.[123]

AI ethics activists can take seriously near-future AI that could drastically increase the power of oppressive institutions. If that seems possible, you might rethink priorities. What's your longer-term game plan? Demanding piecemeal regulation of current misuses may miss the tiger for the mosquitos. Can you envision a positive future for AI? Do you expect to steer us into that, in the face of governments and corporations with vast incentives to ignore, or deliberately create, harmful effects? If not, consider opposing AI outright. You can center the argument that it's plainly unethical to deploy technologies that we don't understand, that are inherently unreliable, and that may drastically harm culture, society, and individual people.

AI safety organizations can call out AI labs' PR pieces about their safety efforts as drastically inadequate. You can advocate for a slowdown or moratorium on research in its current directions. You can advocate for research toward alternative, inherently safer technologies.

I suggest also that the AI safety community should criticize vague utopian promises as misleading advertising hype. If there isn't a plausible specific path to safe AI, we should oppose it outright.

Funders can shift priority from "find a way to make AI safe" to "find ways to halt unsafe AI research, development, and deployment."

Governments can regulate AI, requiring strong evidence of safety before deployment. You can stop funding research that aims to increase AI capa-

---

[122] Seth Lazar's "Legitimacy, Authority, and the Political Value of Explanations" makes a clear case that current AI is politically illegitimate because it is powerful, error-prone, and uninterpretable.

[123] See Kate Crawford's *Atlas of AI* for an overview. AI wielded by oppressive states deliberately harms dissenters and disfavored minorities. AI wielded carelessly by more benign governments and by corporations often does unintentional harm because it doesn't work well, or has unanticipated damaging side effects. Then, because "the artificial intelligence said so"—for uninterpretable reasons—the harmed may lack avenues for redress.

bilities without commensurate safety guarantees. You can fund countermeasures such as those recommended in this chapter.

CREATE A NEGATIVE PUBLIC IMAGE FOR AI

Most funding for AI research comes from the advertising industry. Their primary motivation may be to create a positive corporate image, to offset their obvious harms. Creating bad publicity for AI would eliminate their incentive to fund it.

Shutting down actually-existing AI may seem impossible. I suggest that underestimates resources for doing so, and overestimates resistance.

AI's hype machine deliberately generates the sense of inevitability, of an unstoppable force. It is the belief that AI would be extraordinarily valuable (if only it didn't destroy the world) that makes opposing it seem difficult. However, the public are well aware from watching science fiction movies that AI usually does try to destroy the world, and can be halted only by heroes fighting back.[124]

I suspect AI is a paper tiger, and it can be taken down fairly easily. We just need to create bad publicity—because AI is mostly a publicity stunt itself. It may not be difficult to persuade the public that AI is inherently dangerous and harmful and should be stopped. This requires coordinated political action, but if AI is mainly a public relations stratagem in the first place, government intervention may not even be necessary.

AI has few significant current uses, because the technology is inherently error-prone. It has one dominant application, advertisement targeting. That use depends on another technology, internet surveillance, which the public opposes; shutting that down is feasible and likely, and it may take AI with it.

---

[124]A mid-2023 poll found that "86% of voters believe AI could accidentally cause a catastrophic event, and 70% agree that mitigating the risk of extinction from AI should be a global priority alongside other risks like pandemics and nuclear war." Any poll results should be taken with salt, and opinions might change rapidly if AI has obvious benefits, but this accords with my sense of the public. The Artificial Intelligence Policy Institute, "Poll Shows Overwhelming Concern About Risks From AI as New Institute Launches to Understand Public Opinion and Advocate for Responsible AI Policies," August 11, 2023.

Mooglebook—the advertising industry—provides most of the funding for advanced AI research. Their research projects had long had no clear prospect for profit. The recent spectacular progress in text generation came as a surprise to everyone. Microsoft and Google *have* recently incorporated text generators into multiple products. There are reasons for skepticism about how well that works in practice, and also whether it can generate a profit, taking into account the billions of dollars in sunk investment. This remains to be seen; but counting costs, non-recommender AI research may never be profitable at all. I suspect it is mainly an effort to maintain a good public image. If we sour the public perception of AI, big tech may have no motivation to pursue it.

Internet advertising has a serious public relations problem (and rightly so). As long as AI has a good public image, funding it is good PR. "AI will cure cancer, and we're the ones paying for it!" helps offset "We are spying on your thoughts and using that information to destroy the institutions your survival depends on."

Hyping AI as the shining future creates a dazzling halo effect to make advertising technology companies look attractive to their customers (namely advertisers), to financial markets, to current and prospective employees, and to the public. Just pointing out that most AI research is an advertising industry attempt to improve its reputation may be enough to turn the public against it.

Advertising is most of the business of Facebook and Google, and sizeable chunks for Amazon and Microsoft. They have to convince their customers that internet advertising is worth paying for. Many industry insiders doubt this is true.[125] "We use advanced artificial intelligence for ad targeting, which is why it works so well" is part of the sales pitch.

Many of the AI companies' publicly visible products are shoddy. When users are frustrated with Mooglebook's email service screwing up, it's useful if they think "Well, Mooglebook is full of super geniuses who are curing cancer with artificial intelligence, so email must somehow be much harder than

---

[125] *Hacker News* has a perpetual running argument about this. I find the "doesn't work" position plausible, but don't know enough to have an opinion. Tim Hwang's *Subprime Attention Crisis: Advertising and the Time Bomb at the Heart of the Internet* makes a book-length case. I haven't read it.

it looks." How about spreading the counter-message "you can't trust Moogle-book to deliver your email; why would you trust them with AI?"

AI doomers might seem like natural enemies, but they have been *great* PR because they are true believers in "AI is going to be astoundingly powerful real soon now." They are the most vocal advocates for that, which keeps the hype train running. Now some are saying "we failed, we discovered there is no way to make AI not destroy the universe, we're all going to die." This is awkward for everyone, because destroying the universe might upset the public and be bad PR.

What you can do

So, how can you help shut down AI research with bad publicity? This is extremely not my area of expertise, but here are some speculations.

Probably the relevant expertise is consumer safety activism. This is a large field with an effective playbook that's been applied to automobile safety, food additives, medical devices, toys, and so on. (In some cases, I think the application was misdirected and net harmful, but it is often *effective*.)

The general strategy can aim to create the public perception that AI is inherently sketchy, and that products based on it are unreliable and often harmful. The message might go something like:

> Giant, greedy Silicon Valley corporations are foisting unsafe, untested new technology on the public, and it's harming you right now. The internet is essential to every part of life, and you can't escape the companies that make it. What you *can* do is demand that they remove their creepy "neural" systems, and stop trying to read and manipulate your mind. Like microplastics in your water, these are the insidious, hidden toxins in your phone. We used to have to drive cars that just exploded, until the consumer safety movement forced fundamental changes on Detroit. It's time to do the same for Silicon Valley.

If you are tech person, that may sound manipulative and over the top, but none of it is false.

The movement can also highlight privacy and security, pointing out that Silicon Valley keeps promising them, but actively undermines them instead.

As I suggested earlier, the public is already getting angry about this; tying it in with the anti-AI message is both intuitive and technically justifiable.

Everyone can help spread the word.

Computer professionals understand the problem best, and can lend the authority of expertise to your statements.

If you are a tech person, I'd like to enlist you in saying "Yes, for well-understood technical reasons, it's true that 'neural' networks are inherently unreliable. In my professional opinion, they should be avoided when possible, and limited to uses where getting wrong answers doesn't matter—mostly entertainment." (*Gradient Dissent* explains those reasons.)

Anti-AI messaging might go best as part of a general software consumer safety movement. If you are a tech person, you already know it's way past time for that. Most software *is* shoddy, untested, and risky, and somehow we just put up with it. We bear the costs, not the companies that produce it. We shouldn't. We should demand software that works. That *will* require fundamental changes in the industry, and it will be totally worth it.

Technology executives are not Dr. Evil, and would rather not destroy the universe. Like everyone in the industry, you want to do good, make money, and explore exciting technological frontiers. You can recognize that AI is unfixably unreliable and unacceptably risky, and that your "responsible AI" public messaging is not going to work. Then you can pivot to other innovations.

AI ethics and safety organizations can oppose AI explicitly, and can criticize the Mooglebook labs specifically. You can point out specific ways their research is irresponsible, dangerous to the public, and badly motivated. You can attack their PR statements about their own wisdom and benevolence, and the technological inevitability of a glorious AI future, as the vapid waffle they in fact are.

Funders can direct funds to anti-AI publicity efforts.

Governments can express official concern, doubt, and a generally hostile attitude, leading to demands for accountability, investigations, regulations, and penalties.

Radical progress without Scary AI

Technological progress, in medicine for example, provides an altruistic motivation for developing more powerful AIs. I suggest that AI may be unnecessary, or even irrelevant, for that. We may be able to get the benefits without the risks.

Material progress *matters*. Most people, globally, are enormously better off than we were even only a few decades ago. We have greatly improved health, and longer life span, due to medical advances and increased access. Plague, famine, and war have declined significantly. The majority of the world has instant access to practically all human knowledge and cultural products in our pockets—and wondrous tools for creating and distributing more of it.

In developed countries, nearly everyone takes the fruits of progress for granted, as if they had always already been there, or fell from the sky somehow, or were only grudgingly provided at last by selfish institutions that had previously withheld them. Conspicuously lacking is an awed recognition of the stream of miracles delivered by improved technology and logistics, derived from engineering and science. That's considered politically naive, insufficiently cynical, and as therefore somehow playing into the hands of oppressors.

Most people do not viscerally believe that any further progress is possible. That disbelief, that unwarranted pessimism, is a major impediment to progress itself.

It's *actually possible* to make altogether new kinds of beneficial things—and we should be doing more of that, faster!

Acceleration of progress in science and technology provides a main reason for both hope and fear around Transformative AI. Maybe AI can put an end to old age, sickness, and death. Or, maybe it will produce bioweapons that cause human extinction.

Is it realistic to expect dramatic technological acceleration from AI? I don't think we know enough about either AI or innovation to make a confident prediction.

However, we do know that AI is not the only way to accelerate progress. Others may become available sooner, or may be more effective, or safer. Should we invest more in AI, or in other initiatives? This isn't something we can reason out in the abstract; it requires concrete, evidence-based understanding of what facilitates or impedes progress, and what AI is capable of.

Is it possible to get the benefits of Transformative AI without the risks? My expectation is that dramatic acceleration is feasible *without* Scary AI. I believe a ten-fold increase in science productivity is feasible in the relatively short term. There are many interventions we can apply immediately, and investigation can open up others.

This chapter:

- Discusses the nature of intelligence, and its role in research and development.
- Suggests that technical rationality is not the bottleneck, so automating that with AI wouldn't cause dramatic acceleration.
- Recommends investigating and promulgating other modes of scientific cognition that may be key determinants of progress.
- Observes that the social and cultural contexts for research and development can dramatically help or hinder them.
- Recommends reforming those contexts to remove unnecessary impediments, and to encourage collective creativity.

I mainly discuss scientific research rather than technology development. That's partly because AI futurist discussions generally assume fundamental scientific breakthroughs would enable downstream technological progress. It's partly also because I've read more research on what enables scientific progress than on facilitating technology development. However, my own work experience is as much with engineering as basic research. I believe that what I say about accelerating science mainly goes for accelerating technology too.

The ways we do science now are extremely inefficient, due to incentives enforced by a dysfunctional research environment. We've got pretty good theories of how to fix this; we've confirmed some experimentally, and tests of others are under way.

What would accelerate research, apart from ceasing to actively impede it? What makes it *go fast* when it does? A sudden breakthrough may advance a field more in months or moments than it's managed in decades. What makes those more likely?

Breakthroughs are often attributed to "creative genius" or "intuitive leaps" that are intrinsically beyond any possibility of understanding. I suspect this is a myth that obstructs progress. I believe a better understanding of how science gets done well, and why that works, should give us insight into how to accelerate it. (This is the engineering attitude!) An accurate understanding should come from close observation and interventional experimentation. (This is the scientific attitude!)

Some individual scientists and networks of scientists contribute dramatically more than others. Why? I believe we can discover and understand what great scientists do differently from mediocre ones.

How can we do more of that? I believe we can teach it.

What support environments lead to great science? How are new fields born, how do they get old, sick, or die, and how can they be revivified?

All these are under-studied research questions. Preliminary investigation suggests that better understanding may lead to better outcomes.

This chapter draws from work I've done elsewhere, particularly the essay "Upgrade your cargo cult for the win" and the unfinished online book *In the Cells of the Eggplant*, both on metarationality.com. You can consult them for more details.

What kind of AI might accelerate technological progress?

"Narrow" AI systems, specialized for particular technical tasks, are probably feasible, useful, and safe. Let's build those instead of Scary superintelligence.

"AI" is a famously indefinite term. It means quite different things in different contexts; and, worse, none of those things are clear or specific either. We can't meaningfully address "could AI cause a dramatic technological transformation of everything, and if so when" without *some* clarity about what we're talking about.

"Superintelligent AGI" certainly could accelerate innovation, but only by definitional fiat. It means "AI that is better than humans at *everything*." So, yes, if that were a thing, it would be better at technology development. How much better? Specifically what could it do, how quickly? We have no clue what superintelligent AI would be like, or how it would do research and development differently, so we can't say.

The superintelligence scenario posits a *singularity*: the progress curve goes to infinity. This is a magical solution to all problems; a *deus ex machina* bursting forth from Mooglebook Labs and brandishing a three-step plan:

1. AI.
2. ???
3. Utopia!

That can't be ruled out, but neither can benevolent interstellar aliens showing up and delivering immortality, tasty veggie burgers, and flying cars for everyone. Neither scenario has actionable implications for the present.

We don't know enough about technology development to estimate inherent limits to acceleration, if any. In the paperclip scenario, the AI figured out everything about everything in a few seconds because it was so superintelligent. We can't know whether that is possible, even in principle. However, it seems likely that science and engineering both require conducting inherently time-consuming experiments in the material world, which puts hard constraints on acceleration. Figuring out which are the best experiments to do may save a lot of wasted time, but we don't know how much.

Anyway, superintelligent general AI would probably be bad, so let's not go there, not if we can avoid it. Probably a "narrow AI," meaning one that just did science stuff—or, more likely, many narrow AIs with different specializations—would suffice. That seems safer. Narrow science AIs need not be similar to human scientists, engineers, or mathematicians. Mind-likeness seems unnecessary (and scary).

Since "AI" is such a vague term, it's not clear how "narrow AI" differs from "advanced computer systems" in general. We're already using those in science applications. There seems to be a spectrum of imaginable systems that range from definitely not AI to definitely AI, with intermediate points that are not clearly one or the other.

- Most supercomputer time has been used for arithmetic on large matrices in physics simulations: stress analysis for mechanical engineering, fluid dynamics for weather prediction, n-body mechanics for astrophysics and molecular modeling, and so on. Those are definitely not AI. (Why not?)

- Actually-existing "neural network" AI **just** does arithmetic on large matrices, usually to predict which ads you will click on. That's "AI" but maybe not **Real** AI. (Why is it classified differently from fluid dynamics? From "real" AI?)

- "Neural networks" are already applied, as a data analysis method, to specific scientific problems. (Is this AI? Real AI? Why or why not?) Frequent success announcements support the plausibility of accelerating science with AI, but it turns out that in many to most cases researchers were fooling themselves.[126] The best case so far is AlphaFold, which predicts protein shapes. It includes several sorts of complex domain-specific machinery apart from its "neural" network, including traditional physical simulation. (Does that mean it is not **Real** AI?) AlphaFold is overhyped, but somewhat useful.[127] Generally, I doubt using "neural networks" for scientific data analysis will result in radical transformation, but it's not impossible.

- For decades, AI researchers have built "artificial scientists" which "reason about experiments." These have all been laughably weak. That's because they automate simplistic misunderstandings of what scientists do. Automating a more realistic general understanding of scientific work might count as **Real** AI. However, we don't know much about

---

[126] Sayash Kapoor and Arvind Narayanan give numerous examples in "Leakage and the Reproducibility Crisis in ML-based Science" at reproducible.cs.princeton.edu. See also Elizabeth Gibney's reporting on the problem in "Could machine learning fuel a reproducibility crisis in science?", *Nature*, 26 July 2022.

[127] Derek Lowe, "Why AlphaFold won't revolutionize drug discovery," *Chemistry World*, 5 August 2022.

how humans do science, nor what sort of human intelligence is involved. I'll come back to this later.

- A god-like superintelligence that invents supersymmetric zeptobots would definitely count as Real AI. However, by definition that's impossible to reason about, so there's no point considering it.

WHAT IS THE ROLE OF INTELLIGENCE IN SCIENCE?

Actually, what are "science" and "intelligence"? Precise, explicit definitions aren't necessary, but discussions of Transformative AI seem to depend implicitly on particular models of both. It matters if those models are wrong.

The plausibility of Transformative AI may derive from an implicit belief in *The Scientific Method*: a rational recipe that reliably results in knowledge. Obsolete—but still influential—theories of science imagine it consists of deduction (reasoning about more-or-less formal theories) and induction (relating data and theories). Those are feasible to automate.

In fact, software already has superhuman powers of rationality. Theorem provers (deduction engines) and statistical packages (induction engines) can tackle problems much too large for people, and make no mistakes. Mathematica, a scientific analysis package, knows hundreds of formal methods and gargantuan quantities of specific facts, and can solve in seconds problems that previously required months of human work.

Would a super-Mathematica radically accelerate science? I doubt it. Later in this chapter, we'll see why deduction and induction are only small parts of scientific activity.

There is no Scientific Method, so we can't automate one. No one can explain how or why science works in general, nor how to do it. Philosophers of science proposed various theories in the first half of the twentieth century, but none of them survived comparison with specific instances of good, real-world scientific work. By about 1980, it became clear that there can be no such theory.[128]

---

[128] Part One of *In The Cells Of The Eggplant* explains this in a style intended to communicate to working scientists.

Different sciences work quite differently. Further, each science involves many dissimilar types of cognition and action, which contribute in qualitatively different ways. Major breakthroughs often result from doing science conceptually differently. Conforming to the ritual norms of a scientific community is not sufficient to bring about discovery. Innovative intellectual work addresses the unknown, and so cannot be routinized, ritualized, rationalized, or reduced to any defined method.

"Intelligence" is often thought of as the ability to solve well-specified problems using more-or-less formal methods; i.e., technical rationality. This is also pretty much what IQ tests measure.

According to popular understanding, you have to be unusually intelligent to be a scientist, and superintelligent people are better at it, like Einstein. Presumably that means it consists of difficult thinking, like in an undergraduate science class, where you learn some formal manipulation methods and get tested on whether you can apply them on paper.

Since most people are bad at formal problem solving, and even the most "intelligent" humans can't do it all that fast or reliably, maybe science would go much faster if we automated more of it?

That might be true if solving well-specified puzzles was science's bottleneck, but in most fields it's not. Homework problems from science classes are almost perfectly dissimilar to scientific research. Formal problem solving—technical rationality—is a prerequisite for innovation, but dissimilar to critical aspects of it. Building an AI that can get *perfect* scores on IQ tests is probably easy, and uninteresting because that's not the only kind of intelligence needed.[129]

So what *is* the role of intelligence in science, technology, and material progress, anyway? What sort of "intelligence" matters?

---

[129]Nevertheless, according to the only available data, IQ tests (particularly their mathematical and spatial tasks) do predict future scientific achievement in humans, with a strong correlation holding even at the extreme high end. This is a finding of the Study of Mathematically Precocious Youth. See e.g. Robertson *et al.* "Beyond the Threshold Hypothesis," *Current Directions in Psychological Science* 19(6), 2010, 346-351; and Lubinski *et al.* "Top 1 in 10,000: A 10-Year Follow-Up of the Profoundly Gifted," *J Appl Psychol*, August 2001, 86(4):718-29. There are possible confounds here (expectation effects, for instance); this is the only study of its kind; and it's not entirely clear how to interpret the results, but I think they should be taken seriously. Kaj Sotala discusses implications for AI risk in "How Feasible Is the Rapid Development of Artificial Superintelligence?," *Phys. Scr.* 92 (2017).

A standard Scary AI argument is that we are more intelligent than chimpanzees, and humans are much better at science than chimpanzees, so something more intelligent than us would be much better at science again. But we weren't much better than chimpanzees at science until recently. Human innate intelligence presumably didn't suddenly increase around the time of the Scientific Revolution.

Chimpanzees' cognitive abilities are partly just *different* from ours; less social, in particular. It is culture and the social coordination of work that has made us superior in the past few thousand years, and dramatically more so in the past few hundred. So maybe we need better scientific culture and social coordination, more than IQs of 14,000.[130]

We don't know how much extra scientific ability you get from extra intelligence. Maybe an IQ of 14,000 would make you only a little better at science, even though you'd be *unimaginably* better at the kinds of pointless puzzles IQ tests throw at you. That might be consistent with science being mostly not bottlenecked by unsolved formal problems.

WHAT DO UNUSUALLY INTELLIGENT PEOPLE DO?

If we want to know what a superintelligent AI might do, and how, it could help to investigate what the most intelligent humans do, and how. If we want to know how to dramatically accelerate science and technology development, it could help to investigate what the best scientists and technologists do, and how.

These are shockingly understudied topics. I've found only one systematic investigation of extreme intelligence, the Study of Mathematically Precocious Youth, and it did not ask the relevant question: how are these people thinking? What specifically do they do differently or better than others? Yes, they can visualize rotating geometrical shapes—a typical IQ test problem—but that is rarely a key to success in itself.

Studies of great scientists mainly describe what they achieved (and maybe what else was going on in their lives), but not how. Intellectual

---

[130]Katja Grace made arguments similar to this, and others in this section, in "Counterarguments to the basic AI x-risk case," *AI Impacts*, 31 August 2022.

biographies of single scientists sometimes illuminate their modes of thought, but these are scarce. Comparisons or syntheses are scarcer, and systematic investigations non-existent.

Can whatever it is that great scientists do be taught? I know of no systematic investigations of these topics. They could form a focus area for the discipline of Progress Studies.[131]

Later in this chapter I'll suggest a class of human cognitive activities ("meta-rationality") that seem key to innovation. These are dissimilar to technical rationality (problem solving), although that is a prerequisite. Some people I consider extremely intelligent are outstanding problem solvers. Some not as much; they excel instead at turning real-world situations *into* well-specified problems, thereby making them amenable to technical approaches. Problem identification, selection, and formalization are meta-rational activities. Doing them well is at least important for progress as problem solving is.

AI risk discussions often argue that superintelligences would necessarily seek power without limit, because power is "instrumentally" useful for achieving any goal, and that they would successfully take power because they could use their intelligence to figure out how. This would seem to imply that the most powerful people are among the most intelligent, and that the most intelligent humans seek and gain the greatest power. Neither is true, as far as I can tell, which casts doubt on the premise.

Investigating this may be important in preventing Monstrous AI.

The most powerful people, and notably the most monstrous, are not conspicuously intelligent, at least not in the sense measured by IQ tests. Successful politicians in democracies probably average around one standard deviation above the population; large-company CEOs not too much more, although there are some extremely intelligent ones.[132] Autocratic tyrants seem

---

[131] Patrick Collison and Tyler Cowen, "We Need a New Science of Progress," *The Atlantic*, July 30, 2019.

[132] *Standard deviation* is a statistical measure of distance from the average. On typical tests, "one standard deviation above the population" corresponds to a 115 IQ. Occupational IQ data are uniquely available for Sweden (which may not be representative of other countries, due to population homogeneity). Both CEOs and politicians average slightly less than one standard deviation above the population there. Dal Bó et al, "Who Becomes a Politician?" (NBER Working Paper No. 23120, February 2017); Adams *et al.*, "Are CEOs Born Lead-

generally less intelligent than that (although I know of no studies of this).

Success in gaining power seems to depend instead on extreme Dark Tetrad traits (psychopathy, narcissism, machiavellianism, and sadism). That's moral idiocy, not any sort of intelligence. Maybe we should be more concerned with AI developing superhuman dark tetrad traits than superintelligence.

What is power good for? Why do some people seek it? At a guess, their ego is damaged in a way that makes them crave constant confirmation that it isn't. Is that something we would expect in an AI system?

Why aren't extremely intelligent people extremely powerful? Because they don't want to be, or because intelligence doesn't help gain power beyond a certain point? Or because personal psychology, and/or the social environment actively, differentially disempowers them?

Anecdotally, if you ask the extremely intelligent "why don't you want power," they say "well, then I'd have to tell normies what to do, which means I'd have to talk to them, which would be unbearably tedious." Is that something we would expect in an AI system?

Based on their life choices, it appears that the most intelligent people in the world believe power is *not* useful for what they want to do. If, for instance, you wanted to understand why some cats don't get high on catnip, what would you do with an army of mooks?

"Wait, *what*?" That's the sort of thing extremely intelligent people *do*. The goals of the extremely intelligent are often incomprehensible for outsiders. Scientific and technological progress comes from accepting this, and *getting out of the way* of the sort of people who figure out the optimal method for getting cats high by treating it as a Markov decision process and applying backwards induction on a decision tree using Bayesian linear regression to predict posterior probability of each remaining drug's success probability conditional on previous drugs not working.[133]

Or the sort of person who obsesses about why spinning dinner plates wobble slower than they spin. Richard Feynman's puzzling about *that* led to his figuring out quantum electrodynamics, which is generally considered

---

ers? Lessons from Traits of a Million Individuals" (IFN Working Paper No. 1024, 2014).

[133] Gwern Branwen, "Catnip immunity and alternatives," gwern.net.

a big deal, and the sort of incomprehensible science thing only extremely intelligent people do.

LIMITS TO REASONING, REDUCTION, AND SIMULATION

Most of the doing of science is not reasoning; it is the physical work of experimentation. Therefore, superhuman intelligence might not speed progress much.

Superintelligence scenarios often describe the AI making astonishing breakthroughs by reasoning from first principles, or by short-cutting experimental work by using simulation instead. It can design self-reproducing supersymmetric zeptobots just by thinking hard, and can get it right the first time. If superintelligence axiomatically implies omnipotence, then this may be possible, but that's not actionable information for us.

Otherwise, it's relevant that first-principles reasoning is a very small part of science and engineering, although sometimes an important one. It is relevant that simulation is necessarily imprecise and often inaccurate, so it usually cannot replace experimentation, although it is sometimes valuable.

There's a popular image of scientific geniuses figuring things out by thinking about math in an armchair. Newton and Einstein did that, but the kind of science they did is extremely atypical, and they are misleading as prototypes. Deductive reasoning is sound only when its premises are absolute truths.[134] Newtonian dynamics follow only when Newtonian axioms are absolutely satisfied, and are reliably predictive only when initial conditions are known with perfect precision. Otherwise, they may be unboundedly wrong.

Most of science concerns nebulous messes, not billiard balls on infinite frictionless inclined planes. Cell biology involves nearly no puzzle solving. It is not advanced by theoretical reasoning; it's done in a wet lab. Cells are glop, and there are no glop axioms.

Some AI apocalypse discussions invoke Moore's Law to suggest that arbitrarily detailed simulations will eventually be possible, and faster than run-

---

[134] Part One of *In the Cells of the Eggplant* draws out the implications of deductive absolutism for rationalism and for science in detail.

ning experiments in the real world, and also won't require access to robots or human servants, and that's how the AI gets biological warfare agents.

Most experiments cannot be done in simulation, even with unbounded computation power. The data on which those simulations would be based do not currently exist, and would be extremely difficult to produce. For example, models of biomolecular interactions are limited in accuracy due to insufficient empirical knowledge of the physics of hydrogen bonds and the entropy of solvation. In principle, you could address that with quantum mechanical simulations. However, those are *also* limited in accuracy due to approximations made based on empirical measurements that are also incomplete and imprecise. In principle, you could address that with quantum field simulations at the chromodynamic level. However, quantum chromodynamics is *also* limited in accuracy due to approximations made based on empirical measurements that are also incomplete and imprecise.

Science is empirical all the way down. You never reach a level of deductive bedrock.

Likewise, using AI to cure cancer by reasoning about it would be fantastic, but impossible because human biology is mostly *terra incognita*.[135] Predicting even two-molecule binding is extremely difficult; the relevant physical chemistry is not understood in adequate detail, and data sources that might constrain parameters in empirical models are scant.[136] Predicting all the ways a molecule will interact with the whole human body—toxicity in an unrelated organ, for example—is impossible. We just don't know most of what's going on in there.

There is no way to find out everything a drug candidate will do other than giving it to lots of people and crossing your fingers. That's inherently slow and expensive. It also faces enormous, constantly growing bureaucratic obstacles; clearing those would do far more to speed new medicine than AI.[137]

---

[135] See Derek Lowe's "AI and Drug Discovery: Attacking the Right Problems" (*Science*, 19 Mar 2021)" and Shrager *et al.*'s "Is Cancer Solvable?" (*The Journal of Law, Medicine & Ethics*, 47 (2019): 362-368).

[136] Andreas Bender and Isidro Cortes-Ciriano, "Artificial Intelligence in drug discovery: what is realistic, what are illusions? Part 2: a discussion of chemical and biological data," *Drug Discovery Today*, Volume 26, Issue 4, April 2021, Pages 1040-1052.

[137] Matthew Herper, "Here's why we're not prepared for the next wave of biotech innovation," *STAT*, Nov. 3, 2022.

It seems unlikely that a superintelligent AI could develop biological weapons enormously faster than people can. There's no substitute for killing a lot of monkeys.

LIMITS TO EXPERIMENTAL INDUCTION

Progress requires experimentation. Suggested ways AI could speed progress by automating experiments appear mistaken.

There's a folk theory that you do science by performing experiments, which means measuring a slew of similar things, which produces data, and then a statistics person does an inscrutable Statistics Thing which says that all the data add up to a Science Knowledge, so you add it to the giant pile of Science Knowledges, and when you have enough of those you get flying cars. If that was true, and if AI could do the experiments much faster, we'd get flying cars (or the robopocalypse) much sooner.

There are a couple problems with this: it's not how science works, and there's not much reason to think AI could do experiments much faster. If you ask "isn't it *possible in principle* for a god-like AI to do this," the answer is always "yes, by definitional fiat"; but without a "how" that is meaningless.

Inductive reasoning blesses data as knowledge using formal methods. There is no generally correct way of doing this.[138] A statistical analysis is sound only relative to unavoidable assumptions that cannot be justified rationally; particularly a *small-world assumption* that limits what factors it considers.[139] Those assumptions must be chosen meta-rationally.[140] This means the "artificial scientist" project is quite different from what is usually imagined, and probably much more difficult. We have much less idea how to automate meta-rationality than rationality.

Risk discussions suggest Scary AI would build a vast army of robots to carry out experiments much faster than humans can. Assuming for the sake

---

[138] See "No solution to the problem of induction" in my "Statistics and the replication crisis."

[139] "The probability of green cheese" in *In the Cells of the Eggplant.*

[140] See the "Meta-rational statistical practice" section of "Statistics and the replication crisis" in *In the Cells of the Eggplant.*

of the argument that its manufacturing prowess somehow made that more feasible for it than us, there's not much reason to think it would be useful.

Most wet lab work is inherently serial. You can't know what to do next until you have the results from the experiment you are doing now.

Relatedly, most scientific breakthroughs come from hands-on experimentation; from "getting a feel" for the subject matter. Empirical studies don't just test hypotheses; they are where hypotheses come from.

Large-scale laboratory automation is already in routine use in pharmaceutical discovery, along with advanced statistical methods for interpreting the vast quantities of data it produces. These are helpful, but not magic bullets. Scaling them up by building or buying way more robots is perfectly feasible, and wouldn't be expensive on the scale of pharmaceutical research costs. We don't do that because it wouldn't help much. Robot count is not a bottleneck.

Better robots might help more. On the other hand, it's not clear how AI would be necessary, or even helpful, in creating or making use of them. There's been almost no advancement in practical robot hands for decades, due to mechanical issues rather than AI limitations. And when parallelizing biology experiments, microfluidics difficulties—getting diverse sorts of sticky glop to not gum up tiny tubes—usually exceed robot limitations.

STOP OBSTRUCTING SCIENTIFIC PROGRESS!

We already know how to dramatically accelerate science: by getting out of the way.

Scientific progress has decelerated significantly in recent decades.[141]

---

[141]"Progress" is not easily measured, so this is a somewhat subjective judgement. There are vastly more scientific journal articles published now than in the past, but most seem to have negligible or negative value. In an extensive tweet thread (twitter.com/mattsclancy/status/1612440718177603584), Matt Clancy reviews the evidence for slowing, with citations and graphs. Park *et al.*'s "Papers and patents are becoming less disruptive over time" (*Nature* 613, 138–144, 2023) is a recent quantitative study, summarized in Max Kozlov's "'Disruptive' science has declined — and no one knows why" (*Nature* 613, 138–144, 2023). Classic works are Patrick Collison and Michael Nielsen's "Science Is Getting Less Bang For Its Buck" (*The Atlantic*, November 16, 2018), Patrick

Some of the reasons have become glaringly obvious. The institutional environment for academic science has changed to discourage good work, to reward bad work, and to waste much of researchers' time on activities that have no scientific value or relevance. Off the cuff, I'd estimate more than 90% of resources are wasted now.[142]

Of course, research is inherently uncertain; I don't mean 90% "fails." It would be better if much more research *did* "fail"! Under current incentives, researchers have to ensure that everything they do "succeeds," typically by doing work whose outcome is known in advance, and whose meager results can be stretched out across as many insignificant-but-publishable journal articles as possible. By "wasted," I mean that often even the researchers doing the work know it's of little value. Often they can name better things they would do instead, if they could work on what they believe is most important.

Most resources go into what Richard Feynman called "cargo cult science."[143] We perform rituals that imitate science, but are not science.[144] We are just going through the motions, and that doesn't deliver progress.

Cargo cult science means conforming to misaligned incentives. For academics, it optimizes the proxy objective "publish journal articles," which has increasingly diverged from the actual objective, understanding natural phenomena.

Collison and Tyler Cowen's "We Need a New Science of Progress" (*The Atlantic*, July 30, 2019), and Bloom *et al.*'s "Are Ideas Getting Harder to Find?" (*American Economic Review* 2020, 110(4): 1104–1144). Since those were written, awareness of replication crises across many sciences has made the case even clearer. A recent non-technical statement is Derek Thompson's "Science Has a Crummy-Paper Problem," *The Atlantic*, January 11, 2023.

[142]After writing this off-the-cuff estimate, I came across John P. A. Ioannidis' "How to Make More Published Research True," which estimates 85% of research resources are wasted. *PLoS Med* 11(10): e1001747 (2014).

[143]"Cargo Cult Science," 1974 Cal Tech Commencement address.

[144]Already in 1956, in an outstanding paper on scientific research management, John L. Kennedy and G. H. Putt wrote that "Research has come to be as ritualistic as the worship of a primitive tribe, and each established discipline has its own ritual. As long as the administrator operates within the rituals of the various disciplines, he is relatively safe. But let him challenge the adequacy of ritualistic behavior and he is in hot water with everyone." That's in "Administration of Research in a Research Corporation," *Administrative Science Quarterly*, Vol. 1, No. 3, (Dec., 1956), pp. 326–339.

The safest and most effective way to accelerate progress will be to improve incentives. If 90% of resources are currently wasted on cargo culting, eliminating that might increase research productivity ten-fold.

If we think superintelligence would be immensely valuable, it would also be sensible to make better use of the most extreme intelligences we have now. On the one hand, many of the best science and engineering students get hired by hedge funds and Mooglebook for activities with small or negative net value. On the other hand, those who go into academia face increasing obstacles to getting research done, and an increasingly dismal career path. In the past few years increasingly many of the best have left.

Reversing this will require dramatic changes in incentives. It implies providing outstanding researchers with career paths as rewarding as Bridgewater or Mooglebook, and letting them get on with plate wobbling or tick saliva or zeptobots or whatever other incomprehensible obsession they are on about.

As Stuart Ritchie writes:[145]

> Changes that would make dramatic improvements to the quality of research are *right there*—but, although they're often available, most scientists haven't even begun to pick them up…. The burst of meta-science that we have seen since the replication crisis mustn't be squandered: Pushing for the funding of much more such research should be a major priority for anyone who wants to improve science, and wants to do so using hard evidence.

Some significant changes are already under way. The Open Science and Replicability/Credibility movements, led by scientist-activists, have succeeded in changing some government, university, and academic journals' policies. This has been slow and uphill, but seems to be accelerating, and could reach a tipping point.

Alternatively, impediments may be so entrenched in academia that adequate improvement has become infeasible there. Accordingly, creating alternative, better scientific institutions—funding mechanisms, workplaces, communication channels, social norms—is now important and urgent. Fortunately, this process is also under way.

---

[145]"Rebuilding After the Replication Crisis," *Asterisk*, no date.

I recommend a review article by Matt Clancey, "How to Accelerate Technological Progress";[146] the work of José Luis Ricón on progress studies and reforming scientific institutions;[147] Stuart Ritchie's "Rebuilding After the Replication Crisis";[148] Nadia Asparouhova's post on "Understanding science funding in tech, 2011-2021";[149] and for a deep exploration of possibilities for institutional reform, with many specific proposals, Michael Nielsen and Kanjun Qiu's "A Vision of Metascience: An Engine of Improvement for the Social Processes of Science."[150]

HOW TO SCIENCE BETTER

What do exceptional scientists do differently from mediocre ones? Can we train currently-mediocre ones to do better?

Removing unnecessary obstacles and creating better incentives will encourage people to do science, rather than cargo cult pretend-science. Doing actual science *better*, as well, may yield additional velocity.

We lack specific, accurate knowledge of what scientists do, and why that works. A vague assumption that we *do* know, based on obsolete philosophical misunderstandings, makes investigation seem needless, and so is a major obstacle to progress.[151]

As undergraduates, we learned folk theories of The Scientific Method—derived from long-since disproven early-twentieth-century philosophy—and never noticed they're wrong. We know in detail why a particular biological lab procedure works, but have no idea why science works. We can fix software bugs, but no one can explain what software engineering is.

---

[146]*New Things*, Aug 06, 2021.

[147]Both are on his site *Nintil*.

[148]*Asterisk*, no date.

[149]On her site nadia.xyz.

[150]On scienceplusplus.org.

[151]Part One of *In the Cells of the Eggplant* discusses this at length.

It's assumed that scientists and engineers learn how to do what we do in classrooms and from reading, and therefore our fields are bodies of explicit, codified knowledge. This is false. Key aspects of the work are tacit, and learned only through apprenticeship and personal practice. We know almost nothing about how that works.

We need much more research on what scientists and technologists actually do—not as described in textbooks or even laboratory protocol manuals, but all the parts that *aren't* in there. We need to understand how and when and why the shower thoughts and Slack chats and WTF moments in the lab produce breakthroughs.

Excellence involves types of thinking dissimilar to rational problem solving. The work of science is *meta-rational*, meaning that it is about *how to use rationality*. Doing tasks like these well is critical to scientific progress:

- Find a general topic that is both important and tractable, and choose to work on it
- Understand the state of the art in the area
- Form opinions about what theories are believable (and why) and what issues are important (and why)
- Choose a specific research question
- Define it precisely enough that it's amenable to experiment
- Devise an abstract experimental strategy that could, in principle, answer the question
- Turn the general strategy into a nuts-and-bolts procedure that addresses the messy, nebulous details of the phenomenon and the experimental apparatus
- Perform the procedure correctly; this usually involves extensive tacit hands-on skill, observational acuity, and intuitive understanding— none of which ever gets written down[152]
- Understand the implications of the results
- Explain the experiment and its results accurately and intuitively, so other people in the field understand them too

[152] For one detailed example, see my "Doing being rational: polymerase chain reaction" on metarationality.com.

Experienced technical professionals develop a "feel for" these tasks, which mostly we can't communicate. We have to do this work without a broader or explicit understanding of what it is or why it works.

Some outstanding researchers develop such understanding through critical reflection on the nature of the field. That makes them *better at meta-rationality*: better at figuring out what work is worth doing, and at finding strategies for pushing the whole field forward in that direction. Some can teach this too, multiplying their meta-level understanding through a lineage. Not all scientists considered great have this ability, but perhaps the most valuable scientists are those who do.

Exactly why doesn't cargo cult science work? And what does work? What makes the difference between cargo cult science and the real thing? Institutions can upgrade their norms; but incentives can and always do get gamed.

In "Upgrade your cargo cult for the win" I suggest the antidote is "unflinching lustful curiosity."[153] That means actually wanting to understand what is going on. There is no recipe for finding out, so mindless box-ticking conformity doesn't work.

Curiosity without a set method implies existential commitment: you are accountable to reality itself, not to any specific incentives or objective function. If that is difficult to automate, then we should expect that Transformative AI in Karnofsky's sense may be less imminent or likely than Real AI of other sorts.

Scenius: upgrading science FTW

Empirically, breakthroughs that enable great progress depend on particular, uncommon social constellations and accompanying social practices. Let's encourage these!

(I copied this section nearly verbatim from "Upgrade your cargo cult for

---

[153] On metarationality.com. The "Textures of completion" chapter of *Meaningness* describes this in terms of wonder, curiosity, humor, play, enjoyment, and creation. Sections of the chapter expand on each of those; as of late 2022, only the wonder and curiosity sections are complete. They are highly relevant to scientific practice, I think.

the win" on metarationality.com. There's more there where this came from, if you like it.)

Despite heroic mythology, lone geniuses do not drive most scientific and technological advances. Breakthroughs typically emerge from a *scene*: an exceptionally productive community of practice that develops novel epistemic norms. Major innovation may indeed take a genius—but the genius is created in part by a scenius.

> "Scenius" stands for the intelligence and the intuition of a whole cultural scene. It is the communal form of the concept of the genius.
>
> Individuals immersed in a scenius will blossom and produce their best work. When buoyed by scenius, you act like genius. Your like-minded peers, and the entire environment inspire you.[154]

There is no systematic method for creating a scene, for improving epistemic norms, for conjuring scenius, or for upgrading a community of practice. These are "human-complete" meta-rational tasks. There is no method—but there are methods. There are activities, attitudes, and approaches that encourage scenius. These are available to individuals, institutions, or both.

Communities (including, but not only, institutions) can take a meta-systematic view of themselves. Management theorists describe "learning organizations" that don't base themselves on fixed goals, structures, principles, and procedures. Rather, they hold themselves accountable to reality by conducting continuous meta-systematic reflection on their own commitments, dynamics, and norms, revising those accordingly.[155]

Such reflection may afford much greater leverage than incremental process optimization.

---

[154]"Scenius" was coined by Brian Eno, who wrote the first paragraph of the quote. The second paragraph is from "Scenius, or Communal Genius" by Kevin Kelly, *The Technium*, no date.

[155]At Arcadia, a new scientific research institution, apparently every researcher has two jobs, as a metascientist as well as a scientist. (Seemay Chou, Arcadia CEO, interviewed on *Idea Machines* podcast #47, Sep 1, 2022.) It seems that every scientist is mandated to do the sort of meta-systematic reflection I recommended in "Upgrade your cargo cult" and in "A fully meta-rational workplace" (both at metarationality.com).

Such organizations also foster the learning and development of their members, so they can take on increasingly challenging, interesting, and valuable responsibilities. There are steps an organization can take to transform itself from a cargo cult into a dynamically innovating scene.

Too much of life is wasted going through the motions, playing it by the book, acting according to systems no one really believes in and that fail to reflect a volatile, uncertain, complex, and ambiguous world. This is deadening for individuals, and for society a vast loss of opportunities for prosperity and innovation.

The lesson of cargo cult science for all human activity is that fixed systems are inadequate, because they never fully engage with the nebulosity of reality. We can, and must, upgrade to better ways of thinking, acting, and organizing our communities.

A future we would like

The most important questions are not about technology but about us. What sorts of future would we like? What role could AI play in getting us there, and also in that world? What is your own role in helping that happen?

A better future feels like an unrealistic fantasy from the distant past. For most of us, the future is unimaginable—except to imagine that it will be like the present, but worse. Futuristic AI doom is just one more dystopian scenario on top of pollinator collapse, microplastics, hyperinflation, and—actually—how about nuclear war?

Most progress seems impossible because present-day Mooglebook AI blocks any attempt to make things better. Deploying omnipotent superintelligence may seem like the only way to combat it.

If we free ourselves from AI's malignant grip, we can imagine futures we would like. Flying cars would be fun, but they are not essential. I suggest that most people mostly care about society and about culture.

Society is how we relate to each other and coordinate activities. We would like a society in which we, and most other people, were well-regarded for doing useful things we enjoy, and in which we had reliable supportive relationships.[156]

Culture is how we make sense of questions of meaning, purpose, and value. Those are inherently nebulous but real and important.[157] The future we build depends largely on the sense we make.

---

[156]You might be an exception? I am an autistic hermit and never see anyone and mostly wish society would leave me alone so I'd get more time to write. So I empathize. Nevertheless, I write *for* you, and am glad if you find what I write useful or enjoyable.

[157]I have written parts of a book about this, *Meaningness*, available online.

How AI destroyed the future

We are doing a terrible job of thinking about the most important question because unimaginably powerful evil artificial intelligences are controlling our brains.

"What sort of society and culture do we want, and how do we get that" is the topic of the AI-driven culture war. The culture war prevents us from thinking clearly about the future.

Mooglebook recommender AI does not hate you, but you are made out of emotionally-charged memes it can use for something else.[158]

The culture war's justification for itself is that Americans are profoundly split over fundamental values. This is a lie. Mostly everyone wants the same things; but we can't get them because the Other Side will block any action to bring them about. Everyone urgently wants the healthcare system fixed, but *for exactly that reason* Mooglebook AI whips the Other Side into a frenzy of opposition to any specific proposal, on the basis of some insane theory its human servants invented on the spur of the moment.[159]

During the first few of weeks of covid, it was clear that one side of the culture war would insist that it was an insignificant cold, and the other that it was Doom—but they hadn't yet figured out which side would take which. (Do you remember that the first mainstream left position was that Trump was using covid, an insignificant cold, as a justification for anti-Chinese racism?) This arbitrary inconsistency suggests not a "conflict of values," but Mooglebook AI and its human servants running A/B tests to see which alignment would generate the most ad clicks, page views, and campaign dollars.

Venkatesh Rao writes:

> If we were all in better shape mentally, the way we were in 2006 say, we'd have proper discourses about all this stuff and form coherent mental models and act in a spirit of global mutualism.

---

[158] This riffs on Eliezer Yudkowsky's oft-quoted summary of the risk of AI non-alignment: "The AI does not hate you, nor does it love you, but you are made of atoms which it can use for something else." Making paperclips, for example.

[159] Scott Alexander, "The Toxoplasma of Rage," *Slate Star Codex*, December 17, 2014.

One reason we don't is that it's gotten significantly harder to care about the state of the world at large. A decade of culture warring and developing a mild-to-medium hatred for at least 2/3 of humanity will do that to you. General misanthropy is not a state conducive to productive thinking about global problems. Why should you care about the state of the world beyond your ark? It's mostly full of all those other assholes, who are the wrong kind of deranged and insane.[160]

This is not a future we would like.

What sorts of future would we like? *Not* what we would want. *Not* what is Correct. Not the future in which Our Side wins and "we" get everything the culture war AI has told us we want and deserve to get once we have humiliated the Other Side sufficiently. We're not going to get that.

Realistic futures we would like won't be perfect or Correct. They will be messy and imperfect. They can be better or worse in various respects. What would be, actually, surprisingly nice and pretty good all round?

Imagining a likeable future is a crucial prerequisite to building one. That not easy. You may need to get hostile AI out of your head first.[161]

A ONE-BIT FUTURE

Superintelligence scenarios reduce the future to infinitely good or infinitely bad. Both are possible, but we cannot reason about or act toward them. Messy complicated good-and-bad futures are probably more likely, and in any case are more feasible to influence.

AI is about power and control. The technical details are interesting for some of us, but they're a sideshow.

Superintelligence is a fantasy of power, not intelligence. Intelligence is just a technical detail. Not even that: there is no explanation of what "intelligence" even means there, or what it could do or how. It's arbitrary unspeci-

---

[160]"Ark Head," *Ribbonfarm*, September 29, 2022. Lightly edited for concision.

[161]I suggest methods in "Vaster than ideology," summarized earlier.

fied magic, a *deus ex machina* used to introduce infinite superpower into the plot.

We wanted flying cars, but all we got was 280 characters.[162] Technological progress has ground to a halt (or, that's the feeling). Why?

What's blocking the future are social and cultural dysfunction, not tech. We can't even use the technologies we've got. High speed trains aren't rocket science, but social coordination failures mean America can't deploy them. We've unlocked the technology to make vaccines against all likely future pandemics, and to stockpile them against bioweapons or people messing with bats; but due to the culture war we can't even get adequate funding for broad-spectrum covid vaccines that might end the pandemic permanently.[163]

This makes superintelligent AI attractive to technically-minded people. It's the last open frontier; the last path forward. It would give us the superpower to just wave a wand and *make* the bullet trains run on time, without having to fight the legislature and unions and environmentalists and landowners and regulators and lawyers and "concerned citizens" groups and twitter trolls. We could dominate and disable Mooglebook recommender AI, which controls all those people's brains.

"Whoever develops the biggest AI rules the world" is the ultimate techno-power fantasy showdown.

Superintelligence narratives take power to its logical limit: infinite power by fiat. They imagine extreme scenarios of human omnipotence (deploying AI to exert perfect control over all phenomena), or absolute helplessness under control of omnipotent enemy AI (as slaves, ems,[164] corpses, or paperclips).

Superintelligence makes details of the future inconceivable, by fiat. All the future can get is a one-bit valence: either the AI is a good god and we

---

[162] That's a much-repeated statement from Peter Thiel, a decade ago. The original version was "140 characters," the length limit for Twitter posts at the time; it's now 280 (progress!). He was pointing out that social media had been the most significant twenty-first century technological innovation, which seemed puny compared with twentieth-century progress in material technologies, notably transportation and energy.

[163] I wrote this sentence before the announcement of Project Next Gen, a five billion dollar program to do just this, in April 2023.

[164] "Ems" are digitally simulated copies of individual people's brains. Robin Hanson, *The Age of Em.*

go to an inconceivable heaven, or it is an evil god and we go to an inconceivable hell. In that case, all questions of meaning, purpose, and value reduce to "make sure we get a good god, not an evil one." The simplicity of this moral absolutism may be powerfully emotionally attractive.

Then we try to think up technological means for forcing a god to be good when it would be evil by default ("alignment"). This fails, in part because most candidate solutions, while supposedly technological, follow the logic of narrative—not engineering.

We can fantasize about an AI-granted heaven, but it seems we are all going to hell, and there's nothing we can do about it. The reply to "this is silly" is "well you can't rule out its happening," which is true and important, but it's led to a dead end. We can't use technical rationality to reason about gods.

The future *might* be one bit, but it may be a big complicated mess, the way things have always been. Trying to guess which is more likely isn't helpful.

AI as our only possible savior is a sad failure of the imagination. It probably won't work. We should think of other ways of having a good future.

There are no guarantees for success, but we know lots about how to deal with big complicated messes. We have engineering, and we have politics. They are imperfect, but we can, and should, use both.

COZY FUTURISM

If we knew we'd never get flying cars, most people wouldn't care. What do *we care about?*

I find inspiring José Luis Ricón's vision of cozy futurism:

> *Cool-scifi-futurism* seems almost synonymous with technical advances and feats of engineering: Artificial General Intelligence, nanofabrication, Big Objects In Space, and so forth.
>
> In contrast, *cozy futurism* starts not with technology but with current problems and human needs. You could imagine societies where poverty is absent, housing is affordable, cities are architecturally pleasing, economies are environmentally sustainable, and all disease is cured. Then you work backwards

from there to the technologies, cultural shifts or policy changes needed to get there.

Cozy futurism is not necessarily less ambitious than cool sci-fi futurism: by the time we get to Mars there will still be homeless living among developed countries back on Earth. Nor is cozy futurism just about institutional or cultural solutions. Fusion reactors and anti-aging therapies are key enablers of a cozy future. With cozy lenses on, when envisioning that future you think of what technical advances enable, how they improve our lives; rather than the advances themselves.[165]

Technological progress and a future we'd like are not zero sum, or in conflict at all. Cozy futurism doesn't mean "stop advancing sci/tech," it means "think about what those are for." It means prioritizing advances that make our lives and societies and cultures better.

Is Mooglebook AI making them better? Will AI text generators make them better? Will superintelligence make them better?

AI will probably not be a wish-fulfilling genie that solves all problems. What sort of AI do we want, and why? Concretely, how would it help, in a world we'd like?

Since the 1960s, whenever skeptics ask that, AI enthusiasts say "healthcare!" So far, AI is perpetually "about to" revolutionize medicine, but has delivered very little.[166] The specific longer-term future healthcare applications typically gestured at also do not depend on the sorts of AI currently under development. Specifically what sort of AI would help, how? All-purpose AI as a wish-fulfilling genie is not a likely scenario. All-purpose AI is more likely Doom.

---

[165] Paraphrasing "Cozy futurism," *Nintil*, 2021. I have edited this extract fairly heavily, for relevance and concision.

[166] Dan Elton's "AI for medicine is overhyped" (*More is Different*, Mar 29, 2022) is a sobering debunking by an expert in the field. He explains that the main difficulties, with consequent real-world failures, are due to statistical distributions being quite different in the deployment environment than during training. That is a fundamental, inherent limitation of current AI systems. Visar Berisha and Julie Liss reach similar conclusions in "AI in Medicine Is Overhyped," *Scientific American*, October 19, 2022.

Meaningful futurism

Likeable futures are meaningful, not just materially comfortable. Bringing one about requires imagining it. I invite you to do that!

Cozy futurism is great, but I want to go a step further.

In the same way many people dismiss or are oblivious to the possibility of material progress, many dismiss or are oblivious to possibilities for social and cultural progress. Yet the society and culture of America today are quite different from the ones I grew up in, half a century ago. It's hard to say whether on balance they are better or worse, but having lived that long makes it obvious that *change is possible.*

This goes unnoticed by many, who tacitly assume the world in a few decades can be little different from now. I can see no reason it can't be *much better*, if drop our hip cynicism.

If we knew we'd never get flying cars, most people wouldn't care.

If we knew for sure we'd never get a society in which people mostly get along, and a culture in which mostly people had mostly interesting, enjoyable, *meaningful* lives, we *would* care. We can't be *that* oblivious and cynical.

Meaning is interactional; it's social and cultural; purpose and value are mostly about what you and other people are doing together.[167]

What role can information technology—including AI—play in creating a more meaningful future?

The actually-existing tech industry is mostly about social interaction and cultural consumption. Technology-mediated interaction constitutes increasingly much of our social lives; and the internet delivers most cultural products. In significant ways, that makes our lives richer; but it also leaves many feeling empty, or even nihilistic.[168]

Meaning has been in crisis for the past few decades. Traditional and modern sources both shattered; we live their fragmented, irrational, incoherent

---

[167]"Rumcake and rainbows" in *Meaningness.*

[168]"Atomization: the kaleidoscope of meaning" in *Meaningness.*

wreckage.[169] That has left many of us confused, lost, or even hopeless; others cling to delusional absolutist belief systems.[170]

The culture war feeds on people hungry—desperate even—for meaning and purpose. We find ourselves pursuing tantalizing illusions of belonging and value created by Mooglebook's malignant alien demigods; or doom scrolling in hope of finding meaning in chaos.

I invite you to imagine, in as much detail as you are able, a future you'd like better—and to share your vision, in person and online. This may be the among the most meaningful things we can do.

If you are an AI enthusiast, I especially hope you make a specific case for how AI will lead to a better future. I have looked, and not found any of those—but I am open to the possibility!

Positive visions for AI most often consist of a list of the greatest human complaints, with the unsupported assertion that "AI would fix all these"—somehow. Can you instead imagine how superhuman AI will coexist with humans in a likeable future?

I've sketched a future I would like better in "Desiderata for any future mode of meaningness."[171] It's complicated, yet still short on details, but maybe you will find aspects you like in it too. I suggest a social and cultural mode that provides:

- tradition's sense of secure meaning in community, without its narrowness and material poverty;
- modernity's elegance, effectiveness, and nation-scale institutions, without its oppressive rigidity;
- countercultures' positivity, cultural thickness and breadth, without their anti-rational foolishness;
- diverse and creative subsocieties, without their typically parasitic relationship with the mainstream;
- and our current internet-enabled "atomized" mode's appreciation of nebulosity, and its provision of universal access, without its mindless triviality.

---

[169] I wrote about this in *How meaning fell apart*, on meaningness.com.

[170] "Preview: eternalism and nihilism" in *Meaningness*.

[171] At meaningness.com/fluidity-desiderata.

Will AI help with that? (I wouldn't rule it out… but I'm asking *you*.)

While I was writing this section, Sarah Constantin tweeted a remarkable thread of several dozen "things I'd *like* to see more of."[172] I'd like to see more of most of them too. I think probably most people would. They are meaningful things people do together. They are not dramatic, controversial, or particularly difficult; but they are mysteriously scarce.

Publicizing positive visions *most* people would like seems the way forward. Here are some of the things she'd like, which I'd like too, and maybe you would:

- Group singing (for fun, not by trained singers.) Caroling, ceilidhs, campfire songs.
- Fireworks. Model rockets. Chemistry sets that actually have highly reactive chemicals in them. Just, more recreational explosions.
- Appreciation of normal eighth grade-level American civics. Rule of law, checks on abuse of power, unenumerated rights.
- Hot and cold saunas. Long walks in nature. Moderate use of intoxicants. Spending the afternoon under a shady tree talking with your friends. Juggling, slacklining, frisbee, stuff you do in the park in summer.
- Stories! True, funny, strange stories! Case studies! Anecdotes! All the stories!
- Craft projects. Homemade Halloween and cosplay costumes. Homemade mead and jam. Woodworking.
- Emotional intimacy. Talking about "deep" stuff, how we feel, how our minds work, what we most care about. From a frame of "we're all special snowflakes in different ways and that's fascinating", not necessarily fixing something broken.
- Affection for traditional things (myths, old books, crafts, nature) that doesn't come with constant culture-war zingers about how modernity is terrible.
- LED art, glow sticks and glow-in-the-dark paint, fairy lights, hanging lanterns, candles. Expansion of lighting technology.
- Abundant time to work on passion projects, for kids and adults.

[172]twitter.com/s_r_constantin/status/1578790955519459329.

- Way more industrial automation. More sensors. More robots. No more jobs that ruin anyone's joints or lungs.
- Social groups where you can trust a casual acquaintance with the password to an account full of your money and never worry about it being stolen.
- Archaeology. Only 5% of Mohenjo-Daro has been excavated! We are missing so much information about the ancient world!
- Exciting vehicles. ATVs, jetskis, gliders. Things that make you go "wheee!"
- Stargazing. Treehouses. Even treehouse "cities" like Lothlorien.

Will AI help with those? Maybe! What are the obstacles to our having more of these seemingly pretty easy things?

THE INESCAPABLE: POLITICS

I hate thinking about politics as much as does the next autistic tech geek, but no realistic approach to future AI can avoid questions of power and social organization.

I've suggested that most people like much the same things; yet we are diverse and what we want does differ somewhat. Some conflict is inevitable. Functional politics steers, unsteadily, toward futures more people would like, despite that.[173]

Since preferences are diverse, a main feature of a decent future is that power is adequately distributed. I've emphasized that the danger in AI is that it can (and has) created large new pools of power, faster than counter-vailing checks and balances can be created. In the most extreme scenario, it creates infinite power instantaneously. A one-bit scenario is *perfectly* political: the only possible way forward is to organize society and culture so that no one can, or chooses, to destroy the world. Short of that, consider this, from Samuel Bowman:

---

[173]I've deliberately framed the question as "what sorts of futures would we *like*" rather than "what sort of future do we want." We're not going to get the future "we" want, because wanting is nebulous, diverse, and context-dependent.

Pretty much every bad outcome we're seeing from present-day [AI text generators] could get a lot bigger and a lot worse. In particular, this is enough to get fine-grained surveillance and personalized persuasion to really work: Human-like cognitive abilities—plus cheap compute—would make it possible to deploy the equivalent of one censor or political strategist or intelligence service agent for every citizen in a country. It's easy to imagine ways that even a clumsy implementation of something like this could lead to the rise of new stable totalitarian states.[174]

Checking the power of actually-existing AI can serve as practice, and a testbed, for countering the power of future AI. Mooglebook's AI already reads your emails, and uses that to decide what political propaganda to show you. Do you want that? Are you on board with a movement to make it stop?

If we care about the future, we can't avoid dealing with power, and that means not just "thinking about it" but wielding it. AI people in particular have more power than we realize, and with power comes responsibility.

RESPONSIBILITY

Your scientists were so preoccupied with whether or not they could, they didn't stop to think if they should.
—Dr. Ian Malcolm, in *Jurassic Park*

I have felt it myself. The glitter of nuclear weapons. It is irresistible if you come to them as a scientist. To feel it's there in your hands, to release this energy that fuels the stars, to let it do your bidding. To perform these miracles, to lift a million tons of rock into the sky. It is something that gives people an illusion of illimitable power, and it is, in some ways, responsible for all our troubles — this, what you might call technical arrogance, that overcomes people when they see what they can do with their minds.
—Freeman Dyson

---

[174]"Why I Think More NLP Researchers Should Engage with AI Safety Concerns," NYU Alignment Research Group, October 6, 2022.

> Technologists need to be educated both in how to spot risks, how to respond constructively to them, and how to maximize safety while still moving forward with their careers. They should be instilled with a deep sense of responsibility, not in a way that induces guilt about their field, but in a way that inspires them to hold themselves to the highest standards.
> —Jason Crawford, "Towards a philosophy of safety"[175]

You've heard all this before, and you don't want to hear it again. The quote from the fictional Dr. Malcolm is a pop-cultural cliché. Self-interested entrenched institutions have used "There are Things Man Was Not Meant to Know" to block life-enhancing progress for centuries. It is nearly impossible to advise scientific responsibility without sounding like a morally hectoring junior high school teacher.

Nevertheless, I would urge both AI researchers and AI futurists to consider directions carefully.

AI researchers have tended to dismiss safety concerns, partly because the field moved so slowly, and partly because risks were usually framed in terms of extreme, paperclip-style scenarios. If you have have read this far in my book, you probably believe some concern is now warranted. I suggest that you make that known to your colleagues, and discuss with them possible consequences of the work you do.

Some AI futurists want to create inherently safe superintelligent AI, for the benefits it would bring. I suggest that this is unrealistic, and I recommend reconsidering. If you think superintelligent AI will be a net good, make a specific case for how that's going to work, rather than a handwave like "it will cure cancer, somehow, because superintelligence can do *anything*, and we can probably sort out the safety issues somehow eventually."

Superpower cannot be made safe. Abstract conceptual approaches to alignment have reached a dead end. Training "neural" networks to behave better cannot yield safety, because the technology is inherently unreliable. AI may become safer or less safe, with better or sloppier engineering, but actual safety is out of the question.

The means (technological awesomeness) do not justify the ends (an apocalypse). As safety researchers have pointed out, institutions supposedly

---

[175] *The Roots of Progress*, September 16, 2022.

founded to prevent Scary AI have done more to hasten it than the merely profit-seeking AI labs.

I have felt it myself.[176] *The glitter of artificial intelligence.* It is almost, but not quite, irresistible if you come to it as a scientist. To feel it's there in your fingers, to code up this power that fuels human progress, to make it do your bidding. To perform these miracles, to create superhuman beings out of mathematics. It is something that gives people an illusion of illimitable power, and it is, in some ways, responsible for all our troubles — this, what you might call technical arrogance, that overcomes people when they see what they can do with their minds.

[176]David Chapman, *Vision, Instruction, and Action*, MIT Press, 1991.

This is about you

You are not the monomaniacal monster rationalism imagines you as.
You are almost perfectly dissimilar to "an intelligent agent."

What *you* want is nebulous and context-dependent.
You know better than to go on a quest in search of an ultimate goal.
Discovering what you like is a never-ending path of opening to possibility.

Since you have no fixed purpose, conformity is out of the question.
You participate whole-heartedly in inseparable nebulosity and pattern.

you do not have an "objective function"
you do not have "values"
you do not have an "ethical framework"
your activity is not the result of "planning" or "deciding"

these are all malign rationalist myths
they make you miserable when you take them seriously

you are reflexively accountable to reality
    not to your representations of it
your beneficent activity arises
    as spontaneous appreciative responsiveness

Acknowledgements

My thanks to the generous people who contributed to this work in diverse ways!

This book was prompted and encouraged by funding from the Future Fund Regranting Program. The opinions expressed in it are not necessarily those of the funders, nor of anyone apart from the author, who is solely responsible for errors.

For helpful comments on drafts, and/or other assistance, I thank: Matt Arnold, Charlie Awbery, Gary Basin, Lisa Baues, Gwern Branwen, Tim Converse, Damek Davis, @lumpenspace, @lumpthought, David MacIver, Jake Orthwein, @pachabelcanon, Meredith L. Patterson, Barath Raghavan, St. Rev. Dr. Rev, José Luis Ricón, Josh Rosenberg, Penni Sibun, Kaj Sotala, @strikehigherkey, Lucy Suchman, Anna Ulbricht, Linas Vepstas, Weird AI Luncheon Berlin (rikard hjort, nick stares, Sean j, fey.chu), and several people who prefer not to be named. Many others have been helpful in Twitter conversations; I apologize for not tracking those.

Super extra thanks to @lumpenspace for proposing major, necessary rethinkings of the book's audience, purpose, structure and contents; and for detailed comments on 239 drafts.

Gradient Dissent

Summary of Dissent

The neural network and GPT technologies that power current artificial intelligence are exceptionally error prone, deceptive, poorly understood, and dangerous. They are widely used without adequate safeguards in situations where they cause increasing harms. They are not inevitable, and we should replace them with better alternatives.

Gradient Dissent is divided into three chapters, plus an epilogue.

- "Artificial neurons considered harmful" explains how and why neural networks are dangerously unreliable.

- "Backpropaganda: anti-rational neuro-mythology" explains the misleading rhetoric decision makers use to justify building and deploying dangerously defective AI technology.

- "Do AI as science and engineering instead" discusses neglected technical approaches that may make systems based on neural networks less risky. Ultimately, though, those cannot be made adequately safe with technical fixes; nor can technical progress address irresponsible misuse. Instead, these technologies should be deprecated, avoided, regulated, and replaced.

- Neural networks have dominated AI for only a decade. They are not mandated in some Cosmic Plan. The brief epilogue, "A better future, without backprop," suggests that it's important, urgent, and probably possible to replace them with better alternatives.

Gradient Dissent is a companion document for *Better without AI*. It goes into more detail than some readers would want, so I have separated it out from the main book. It also is self-contained, and you can read it on its own, if you are more interested in the technologies themselves than in the ways they may interact with society (the main book's topic).

Reading *Gradient Dissent* requires no specific technical background. It neither assumes you know how neural networks work, nor does it contain an introductory explanation that would get you up to speed. You can understand it without knowledge of those details. If you run into technical bits that seem difficult, you can skim or skip over them without missing much.

Artificial neurons considered harmful

So-called "neural networks" are extremely expensive, poorly understood, unfixably unreliable, deceptive, data hungry, and inherently limited in capabilities.

In short: they are bad.

Lies, damned lies, and machine learning

Many confusions result from the vagueness of the terms "statistics," "machine learning," and "artificial intelligence." The relationships between these are unclear and have shifted over the years.

Traditional statistical methods have the virtue of simplicity. It is comparatively easy to understand what they do, when they will work, and why. However, the circumstances in which they do work are quite restricted.

Traditional statistical methods come with mathematical guarantees: if certain conditions hold, the output of a particular sort of statistical analysis will meaningful in a particular way. Those conditions almost never do hold in the real world, so statistical analyses are almost never "correct." As a result, it is easy to fool yourself, and others, with statistics.[177] Good use of statistics requires *meta-rational judgement*: informal reasoning about whether a method, whose use is formally mistaken, may give adequate guidance for particular

---

[177] Hence, "lies, damned lies, and statistics"—attributed to Mark Twain. Also *How to Lie with Statistics*; and see "Statistics and the replication crisis" at metarationality.com/probabilism-crisis.

purposes in a particular context.[178] It also requires on-going monitoring, after a method is put into routine practice in a particular context, to keep checking whether it is working well enough.

These requirements are not widely understood, so traditional statistical methods are often misused. Sometimes that has catastrophic consequences, as in the 2008 Great Financial Crisis and in the current medical science replication crisis.

Machine learning was once considered a small subfield within artificial intelligence. During the 1990-2000s AI Winter, machine learning split off as a separate field. It studied statistics-like data analysis methods that lack theoretical justification. It mostly avoided reference to artificial intelligence. Recently, "artificial intelligence" has come to be seen as a subfield within machine learning.

"Machine learning" methods are applicable to "messy" or "complex" datasets, meaning ones without the simple properties required to make traditional methods work. In this sense, they are "more powerful." However, there's no general reason they ought to work when they do, so it's difficult to guess whether they will be adequate for particular uses.

It is also difficult to tell *whether* they are working. With traditional statistical methods, there are principled ways of checking adequacy and understanding failures. Machine learning practice substitutes a purely empirical test: how well does a model predict data collected—perhaps haphazardly—in the past?[179]

That is justifiable only if future data will be sufficiently similar to that already collected. It may be difficult or impossible to reason about whether that will be true. It is hard to know what the future will be like even in general; and what measure of "similarity" is relevant depends on the specific task and specific model.

This makes it even easier to fool yourself with machine learning than with traditional statistics. It implies that responsible use requires near-paranoid distrust, and still greater commitment to on-going monitoring of accuracy.

---

[178]"All models are wrong, but some are useful" was the way George Box famously put it, in "Science and Statistics," *Journal of the American Statistical Association* 71:356, 1976.

[179]A strong, historically important justification for this practice is Leo Breiman's "Statistical Modeling: The Two Cultures," *Statist. Sci.* 16(3): 199-231 (August 2001).

NEURAL NETWORKS AND ARTIFICIAL INTELLIGENCE

"Artificial intelligence" is currently almost synonymous with applications of a single method, *error backpropagation*. That is a statistical method misleadingly described as "neural networks" or "deep learning." Backpropagation is currently applicable to tasks amenable to no other known method, but suffers major drawbacks.

"Neural networks" are even more difficult to reason about than other machine learning methods. That makes them power tools for self-deception. Mainly, researchers don't even try to understand their operation. The "Backpropaganda" chapter explains how they justify that.

I often put "neural networks" in scare quotes because the term is misleading: they have almost nothing to do with networks of neurons in the brain. Confusion about this is a major reason artificial "neural networks" became popular, despite their serious inherent defects. I will often refer to them as *backprop networks*, for that reason.[180] ("Backprop" is a common shorthand for "backpropagation.")

The upcoming "Engineering fiasco" section argues that using them is often irresponsible. They should be restricted to applications in which other mechanisms provide safety backstops, and as much as possible should be avoided altogether.

Traditionally, the machine learning field treated neural networks as one method among many—and not usually as the leading technique. However, they are now considered more powerful than any other known method, in being applicable to a wider range of data. Recent progress with backpropagation has led many researchers to believe it is capable of realizing the dream of advanced artificial intelligence. AI is now taken to be a subset of its applications.

Equating artificial intelligence with backpropagation creates two sorts of distortions. Statistical methods (including backpropagation) are inherently limited in ways that people (and some other AI methods) aren't. And, many applications of neural networks don't reasonably count as AI. When I express skepticism about applications of artificial intelligence, people often cite applications of neural networks instead.

---

[180]"Backprop network" is a common usage, but may also be misleading, because backpropagation is not involved in the operation of the network itself.

Neurofuzzy thinking

To illustrate the non-equivalence, rice cookers are an extreme example. Some of these inexpensive home kitchen appliances contain neural networks. According to the manufacturer Zojirushi, who brands them as "neurofuzzy," that "allows the rice cooker to 'think' for itself and make fine adjustments to temperature and heating time to cook perfect rice every time." This is "thinking" or "intelligence" only in the loosest, most metaphorical sense.

Although I lack expert knowledge of rice cooking, I expect well-understood traditional control theory methods would work as well as a "neural network." Those would be simpler, and they come with mathematical guarantees that would give reasonable confidence that they'd work.

I expect the rice cooker designers weren't idiots, and understood this. So why did they use a neural network?

- Presumably it's largely marketing hype.
- Maybe it isn't even true; quite often companies claim to "use AI" when they don't at all. It helps create a positive public image.
- Maybe there *is* a "neural network" in there, because marketing people decided that would sell it, and they told the engineers to put one in.
- Or maybe it was more fun for the engineers to use a sexy "artificial intelligence" method than boring old control theory.

If the rice cooker *does* have a neural network, I expect it's a very small one. I expect the designers either hand-wired it, or they reverse engineered it from the results of a "machine learning" process, making sure it does something sane.

I also expect they put safety mechanisms around the neural network. Those would ensure that, regardless of whatever the neural network does, the cooker won't explode. These are the precautions everyone *ought* to apply before using neural networks for anything more than entertainment.

Revolutionizing what, specifically?

It's common to read that "applications of artificial intelligence are revolutionizing a host of industries," but on examination it turns out that:

- most practical applications don't involve anything most people would count as "intelligence"

- most are not revolutions technically or economically; many have smaller total addressable markets even than rice cookers
- many are unsafe and irresponsible
- many might work better using some better-understood, more reliable method than neural networks.

In most situations, well-understood traditional statistical methods, or machine learning methods that are less expensive and more understandable, work better.[181] Plausibly, many times when people try backpropagation first (misguided by hype), and it works well enough to get put into use, alternatives would have worked better. When backpropagation succeeds quickly, it may be because the problem is trivial: for example, nearly-enough piecewise linear. In such cases, backpropagation is expensive overkill.

For some tasks, however, backpropagation can produce astounding results that no other current method can approach.

Gradient Dissent explains the inherent risks in using backpropagation, suggests ways of ameliorating them, and recommends developing better alternatives.

BACKPROP: AN ENGINEERING FIASCO

Backpropagation requires masses of supercomputer time, is difficult or impossible to get to work for most tasks, and is inherently unreliable—and therefore unsafe and unsuitable for most purposes.

From an engineering point of view, "neural" networks are awful:

- **Inefficient**: They are extremely computationally expensive.

---

[181]When investors or senior management tell a clueful technical team to solve a problem with "AI," often the engineers use something simpler, cheaper, and more reliable than backpropagation; then report success; and the company touts its "AI solution" to the public. This practice is common enough that the US Federal Trade Commission issued a warning in February 2023 that they would take action against it: "Keep your AI claims in check." Relevant are Amy A. Winecoff and Elizabeth Anne Watkins' "Artificial Concepts of Artificial Intelligence" (*arXiv*:2203.01157v3) and Parmy Olson, "Nearly Half Of All 'AI Startups' Are Cashing In On Hype" (*Forbes*, Mar 4, 2019).

- *Difficult to make work*: Getting adequate results in new real-world applications is often impossible, and usually takes person-years of work by expensive specialists if it succeeds.
- *Unreliable*: Backprop networks are unavoidably, unfixably unreliable, and therefore unacceptably unsafe for most applications.

The next few sections explain why.

We would reject any other technology that violated basic engineering criteria so completely. "Backpropaganda," the second chapter of *Gradient Dissent*, explains some reasons—bad ones—tech companies make an exception.

But, it's also true that backprop networks can sometimes do things that no other current technology can do *at all*. Even if they usually do them badly, some outputs are astonishing. That is what makes current AI exciting. Most of the time the image generator DALL-E doesn't give you what you asked for, and getting it to give you exactly what you want is usually impossible. With a lot of work, though, it may eventually give you something close enough for your purposes; and also many of the totally wrong things it gives you are *amazing*, even if people in them have six fingers. This is fantastic for a toy, and for demo hype, perhaps for commercial illustration generation if someone counts fingers before publication, and unacceptable for engineering applications.

Since backprop networks are inherently unreliable, they should be used only as a last resort, and only when:

1. Bad outputs are not costly, risky, or harmful; or
2. Each output can be checked by a competent, motivated human; or
3. You can drive the error rate so far down that bad outputs nearly never occur in practice, *and* you have justified confidence that this will remain true in the face of the volatility, uncertainty, complexity, and ambiguity of the situations where the system will be used.

Fortunately, most deployed systems do fit one of the first two categories (and often both). (*Deployment* means "putting into regular use.") For instance:

- Backprop networks are used for image enhancement in digital photography; when they screw up, it's usually either obvious to the photographer or inconsequential

- Image generators such as DALL-E are for entertainment and aesthetic purposes only, and therefore mostly harmless—so far. (There are increasing concerns about fake photos and videos used in scams and propaganda, and about job losses for artists and photographers.)

- The outputs of program synthesis systems such as Copilot are useful although unreliable, so they depend on expensive, highly-trained experts (software engineers) to check and correct each output.

I'm not sure there are any applications in the third category; the next section explains why.

DO NOT connect artificial neurons to heavy machinery.[182]

Unfortunately, idiots *do* connect backprop networks to heavy machinery, metaphorically speaking at least, and that should be condemned. Applications in policing, criminal justice, and the military are particularly concerning. Sayash Kapoor and Arvind Narayanan's "The bait and switch behind AI risk prediction tools" discusses several other interesting real-world examples.[183]

The internet is, in some metaphorical sense, the heaviest machinery we've got. Connecting text generators to it has several potentially catastrophic risks (discussed in "Mistrust machine learning" in *Better without AI*). So far, the only significant harm has been the swamping of the web with AI-generated spam. That has made Google Search much less useful than it had been. Ironically, one of the main uses for ChatGPT has been as a web search replacement.

---

[182] Automobile driver-assist systems may be an exception—not full self-driving, but the much more limited versions that have been in routine use for several years as of 2023. Arguably those meet all three criteria I listed for safety. They are limited to taking actions (braking and lane-keeping) that are relatively unlikely to be catastrophic even if triggered mistakenly; their error rate has been driven down a long way; they can be overridden immediately, and their outputs must be continuously checked by a competent, motivated human, i.e. an alert driver. Nevertheless, they do sometimes cause fatal accidents, and many drivers choose to disable them.

[183] *AI Snake Oil*, Nov 17, 2022.

BACKPROP NETWORKS ARE DECEPTIVE

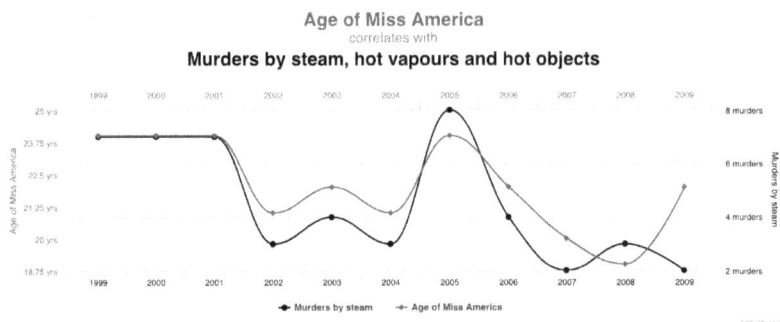

Backprop networks frequently fool their creators into believing they can do things they can't. This is not due to deliberate intent on their part. It's due to non-obvious properties of statistical behavior that are hard to detect and hard to overcome.

Backpropagation is a method of *training* a network to perform a particular sort of prediction by presenting it with a set of known-correct input/output pairs. These are called the *training data*. After training finishes, the network can be put into use, where it is supposed to predict outputs corresponding to new inputs. Recommender AIs predict whether you will click on an advertisement. GPTs, the technology powering text generators, predict a natural-sounding response to your prompt.

Backpropagation frequently finds ways of "cheating" by exploiting *spurious correlations* in the training data. Those are accidental patterns that show up consistently in the training data, but that don't hold true where the network will be used. (The chart above is a funny example.[184]) It is often easier for backprop to find a spurious correlation in training data that only accidentally "predicts" the past than for it to solve the problem the creator cared about.

When backprop exploits spurious correlations, it may give excellent results during training—and fail catastrophically when put into use. Unfortu-

---

[184]The chart is by courtesy of Tyler Vigen under the Creative Commons Attribution 4.0 International license at tylervigen.com/spurious-correlations.

nately, it can be extremely difficult to determine *whether* it has deceived you in this way; and it can be extremely difficult to prevent it from doing so.

Here's a simplified example. If you want a supermarket warehouse AI that can tell whether something is a banana or an eggplant, you can collect lots of pictures of each, and train a network to say which ones are which. Then you can test it on some pictures it hasn't seen before, and it may prove perfectly reliable. Success, hooray!

But after it's installed in a supermarket warehouse, when it sees an overripe banana that has turned purple, it's likely to say it's an eggplant.

If you had no overripe banana pictures in your original collection, you'd never notice that backprop had fooled you. You thought it learned what bananas looked like, but it only learned to output "banana" when it saw yellow, and "eggplant" when it saw purple. It found a spurious correlation. That was a pattern that held in the training data as an accidental consequence of the way they were collected, but that doesn't hold reliably in the real world. The problem it solved was easier than the one you wanted it to solve, so that's what it did.

This type of failure occurs *almost always*. Detecting it, and finding workarounds, is much of the work of building practical AI systems.

THE LIMITS OF INTERPOLATION

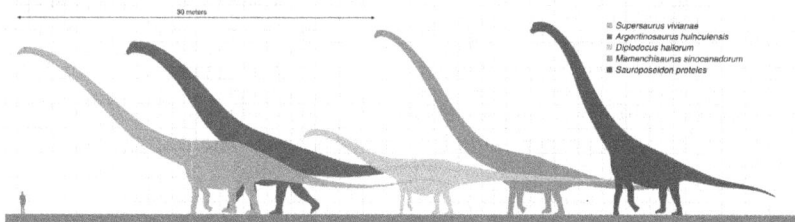

Backprop networks work by interpolation: guessing answers based on similar cases in its training data. They are inherently unreliable when given inputs unlike any they were trained on.

Network training is metaphorically similar to learning how things are likely to go based on experience. The training data are like past experiences.

They are situations (inputs) together with their results (outputs). Recommender AIs are trained on databases of past events in which people with particular traits did or didn't click on particular ads. Text generators are trained on databases of bits of previously-written text and what came next.

"Interpolation" means guessing, when given a particular input that is *not* in the training data, that the correct output will be similar to the training outputs for the most similar training inputs. For example, paleontologists can estimate the length of sauropod dinosaur species from a single femur, if that's the only fossil bone found.[185] For some other species, there are complete fossil skeletons of known total length and femur length. Given a new femur 2.0 meters long, it's reasonable to estimate a total length of 20 meters, based on the nearest two species, one with a 1.5 meter femur and 15 meter total length, and another with a 2.5 meter femur and 25 meter total length. This is a linear interpolation—you just draw a line between (1.5, 15) and (2.5, 25), and find where 2.0 lies on it.[186]

Some people dismiss backprop networks as **just** doing interpolation. This is a mistake, however: the word "just" minimizes what interpolation can do. Networks interpolate based on "similar" training data; but similar how? In the case of femur lengths, "similar" is just numerical closeness.[187] But what makes two sentences similar? "The quokka bit the mayor" is similar to "The mayor bit the quokka" in one sense, and similar to "The head of the town council was savaged by an illegal pet marsupial" in another. How would you rate those similarities numerically?

Finding a *task-relevant* measure of similarity accounts for backpropagation's power. Training creates a *"latent space,"* in which numerical closeness equates to similarity for prediction. "The quokka bit the mayor" and "The mayor bit the quokka" have identical words in a slightly different order. However, the distance between them in a text generator's latent space should be

---

[185]The sauropod length diagram above is by courtesy of user KoprX under the Creative Commons Attribution-ShareAlike 4.0 International license at https://en.wikipedia.org/wiki/Dinosaur_size#/media/File:Longest_dinosaurs2.svg.

[186]I picked round numbers to make the answer easy to see, but these are approximately accurate. Sauropods did get quite long and it would be fun to revive some if that becomes possible.

[187]The diagram of sauropod length interpolation above is by courtesy of Matt Arnold (personal communication).

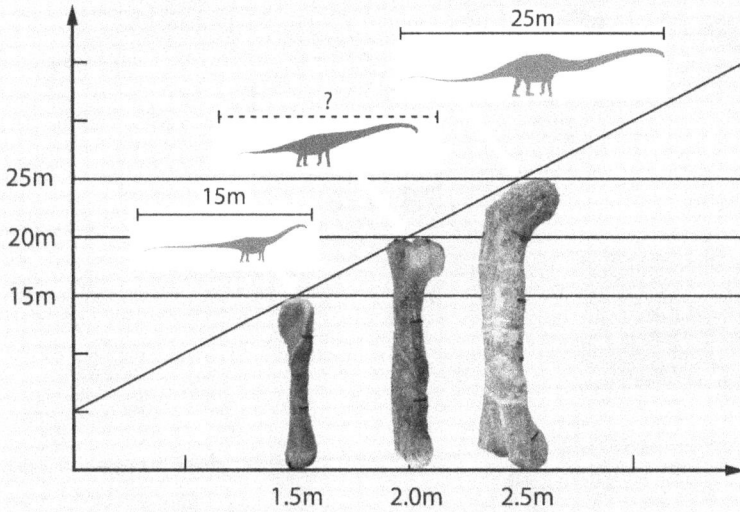

large, because what follows is likely to be quite different. On the other hand, "The head of the town council was savaged by an illegal pet marsupial" should be quite close to "The quokka bit the mayor," even though they share only one word. The sentences mean much the same thing, and can plausibly be followed by most of the same things.

Backprop networks "just" do linear interpolation in latent space. But the results can seem like magic, or at least "intelligence," if training manages to get *meaningfully* similar inputs close to each other in latent space. You can think of the latent space as *abstracting* a task-relevant ontology of categories from apparent features. That predicts task-relevant similarity.

Then it is apparent that good performance requires dense sampling *in the latent space*. Latent space is unimaginably huge and weird. Interpolation is linear, but latent space is highly nonlinear. Superficially similar inputs may correspond to very different places in latent space (as with swapping the quokka and the mayor).[188] Given a new prompt, unless there was some training input that was nearby in latent space, the network's output will likely be

[188] The diagram of paths through the backprop network above is by courtesy of Matt Arnold (personal communication).

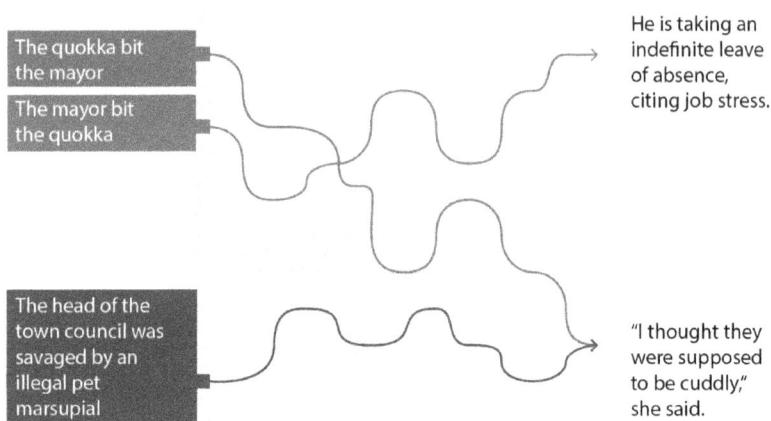

nearly random. This is why backprop depends on "big data"—vastly more than people require to learn anything.

To get a sense of latent space, check out the YouTube video "Latent Space Walk."[189] It "walks" through a tiny bit of the latent space of an image generator network. Each point in latent space corresponds to a complete image. Each frame in the movie is generated from a single point in latent space. Each next frame is generated from a latent space point close to that of the previous one. So, following a path through latent space, generating a new image at tiny regular intervals, produces a shifting series of seeming landscape paintings, in a consistent style, but with gradually changing contents.

Depending on how abstract and meaningful the latent space is, "just" interpolating can be extremely impressive. Some people equate abstraction ability with intelligence itself. I think that's not usually a good way of understanding it, but it's not silly either.

Another latent space walk, at youtube.com/watch?v=YnXiM97ZvOM, takes you through a part of the space based on headshots. The moving tiny x in the right-hand pane shows the path taken through the space. You can see in the left-hand pane how the network has abstracted meaningful facial qualities from its training data.

---

[189] At youtube.com/watch?v=bPgwwvjtX_g

Nevertheless, by Occam's Razor, we should assume as little abstraction as necessary to explain a network's behavior. We should expect that, typically, outputs are similar to ones in a training example, or a few training examples stitched together.

This usually seems to be the case for both text and image generators. It's amazing how *well* they work, but a general sense of *how* they work is not extremely mysterious when examined. The "how well" depends on mind-boggling quantities of training data—enough to fill the latent space. Current text generators ingest trillions of words in training, equivalent to tens of millions of books. Our intuitions about how smart they are get distorted because we literally cannot imagine what it would be like to have read and memorized that much.

It's also not mysterious how badly backprop systems work sometimes. Similarity in their latent space is only intermittently similar to our notions of similarity. If you ask DALL-E for a photorealistic image of Vladimir Putin rollerskating in Red Square, you may get something that is astonishingly like that, *except* that he has three legs. We think having three legs makes someone extremely dissimilar to Putin, but image generators don't. (That is why they work best for surreal fantasy scenes.)

BRITTLENESS OUT OF DISTRIBUTION

Some good arguments against the possibility of inherently safe AI turn on the real world situation in which a system is used being significantly different from its training data. Then it will encounter *out of distribution* inputs, things unlike those it has seen before, and its behavior will be inherently unpredictable—no matter how well-behaved it was during training. It will be forced to extrapolate, not interpolate.

We can form a somewhat deeper understanding of the "purple banana" problem in terms of the limits of interpolation. What would be a good dinosaur length estimate if you found a 7 meter femur? This is termed an "*out of distribution*" input: nothing anywhere near that big has been recorded previously. You could scale up linearly and estimate 70 meters, but you'd probably be wrong.

In this case, the linear estimate would not be an interpolation (*between* known cases), but an *extrapolation* (*outside* the range of known cases). Extrapolation is highly unreliable. It's likely that a dinosaur with that dissimilar femur had a dissimilar body shape as well: proportionately longer legs, maybe for a different gait, evolved for different terrain.

Any method that works by interpolation is vulnerable to this critique—although mainstream statistical methods fail in ways that are better understood, and therefore easier to mitigate against, than those of machine learning.

On this basis, we should expect poor network performance when there's nothing relevantly similar in its training data. We should assume any AI system using statistical methods will be unsafe in open-ended real world situations, which are vastly weirder and more complicated than any training data set.[190] And, this has been the common experience.[191]

This makes me skeptical of "alignment" approaches based on "training" backprop networks to behave well. *Reinforcement learning with human feedback* (RLHF) uses standard machine learning methods to prevent text generators from producing outputs considered "bad"—because they are offensive or unhelpful, for instance. It trains an existing generator on a database of "good" and "bad" user interactions.

RLHF has been critical for the success of ChatGPT and similar systems, because negative PR from "bad" outputs had been a major obstacle previously. (Recall from "Create a negative public image for AI" that AI was, and arguably still is, mainly a PR strategy for the advertising industry.)

RLHF is further positioned by chatbot providers as an alignment method for AI safety, which is disingenuous. It addresses the most publicized, but least significant, AI ethics concerns. It does not address AI safety—in the sense of "make sure it doesn't kill people"—at all. So far, it

---

[190]An excellent discussion, with policy recommendations, is Ganguli *et al.*'s "Predictability and Surprise in Large Generative Models," *arXiv*:2202.07785v2, 2022.

[191]"Models that achieve super-human performance on benchmark tasks (according to the narrow criteria used to define human performance) nonetheless fail on simple challenge examples and falter in real-world scenarios. A substantial part of the problem is that our benchmark tasks are not adequate proxies for the sophisticated and wide-ranging capabilities we are targeting: they contain inadvertent and unwanted statistical and social biases that make them artificially easy and misaligned with our true goals. We believe the time is ripe to radically rethink benchmarking." Kiela *et al.*, "Dynabench: Rethinking Benchmarking in NLP," *Proceedings of the 2021 Conference of the North American Chapter of the Association for Computational Linguistics*, pp. 4110–4124, June 6–11, 2021.

seems that chatbots are not a serious AI safety risk. However, describing RLHF as an alignment method may cause unwarranted complacency. Although RLHF makes "bad" outputs much less likely, chatbots still frequently produce them.[192]

Like all machine learning methods, RLHF is inherently unreliable, only probabilistically effective, and should not be used when "bad" outputs can be seriously harmful. Even if you drive the probability of badness down to levels you consider acceptable during training, bad behavior in the real world remains unboundedly likely, due to the distributions of inputs differing from those in the training data. Nobody can think of all the bad things an AI system might do, in order to train it not to.

Engineering often aims for *graceful degradation*. When a machine fails, due to internal breakage or because its environment is not as expected, it should either grind to a gradual stop, or continue to operate but less well. It should not explode, melt down, or spew toxic chemicals. Text generators often do not degrade gracefully; when they fail, it can be by spewing deceptively plausible falsehoods, absurd nonsense, or toxic language.

Is it feasible to get them to just notice when an input is out of distribution and refuse to proceed? As with the previous approach, this might help somewhat, but if the noticing method is also based on backprop, it won't be reliable either. And, its similarity metric will be somewhat bizarre ("person with three legs looks like Putin"), so its idea of what's out of distribution will be off.

The opposite of graceful, gradual degradation is often termed "brittleness." A brittle material doesn't bend under stress; it suddenly shatters.

Brittleness is an obstacle to deployment, if it's taken seriously. This is good, if you assume by default that any new AI system is dangerous and shouldn't be deployed (as I do). Brittleness is bad, if you expect idiots to nevertheless connect it to heavy machinery (as they do).

---

[192] Casper *et al.* provide a useful survey of reasons for the inherent inadequacy of RLHF in "Open Problems and Fundamental Limitations of Reinforcement Learning from Human Feedback," *arXiv*:2307.15217v2, 2023.

Beyond interpolation: reasoning?

So if people are "really" intelligent, how do we deal with stuff "way out of the training distribution"? In other words, situations unlike any we've seen before?[193] What do we do that isn't mere interpolation?

The standard answer is that we apply reasoning. We can use a chain of deductive or causal logic to figure out a correct answer to a novel problem, or an effective course of action in a novel situation. For example, we might suppose that scaling up a sauropod linearly to 70 meters is implausible because weight grows as the cube of length. We might, further, reason about different body plans that could accommodate a 7 meter femur. We might use mechanical engineering stress analysis techniques to check their plausibility.

Many researchers assert that backprop networks don't, and maybe can't, reason logically, which is why they aren't **really** intelligent. So, they say, that needs to get fixed somehow—either by coupling the backprop network with a logical reasoning system, or by training the network to reason itself.

This seems dangerous. Backprop networks that flail about more-or-less randomly when they encounter novel situations are bad, but they will destroy the world only by accident: if some idiot connects them to nuclear weapons or to internet advertising platforms or something. That would be unfortunate, but maybe other people will have enough sense to stop them. AI systems that act *competently* out of distribution are liable to destroy the world on purpose. This is a Scary scenario.

We don't want AI systems trying to be rational unless we're confident they will do a good job. "Good" here must be morally as well as cognitively normative. Backprop-based systems probably cannot be reliably rational (in part because they can't be reliably *anything*). If they are "trained" into more nearly approximating rationality, and deployed with the expectation that they will be consistently rational, disaster seems likely.

---

[193]There are definitional problems here. What counts as "way out" or "unlike"? These are meaningful only relative to some measure of similarity, for which there is no objectively correct choice. "In distribution" is somewhat conceptually incoherent unless it means "identical to an item in the training data." It's metaphorically useful, however, so we can ignore the issue for the purpose of this discussion.

Backpropaganda: anti-rational neuro-mythology

Current AI results from experimental variation of mechanisms, unguided by theoretical principles. That has produced systems that can do amazing things. On the other hand, they are extremely error-prone and therefore unsafe. **Backpropaganda**, *a collection of misleading ways of talking about "neural networks," justifies continuing in this misguided direction.*

Two dangerous falsehoods afflict decisions about artificial intelligence:

- First, that neural networks are impossible to understand. Therefore, there is no point in trying.
- Second, that neural networks are the only and inevitable method for achieving advanced AI. Therefore, there is no reason to develop better alternatives.

These myths contribute to the unreliability of AI systems, which both technical workers and powerful decision-makers shrug off as unavoidable and therefore acceptable.

A natural question after learning that current AI practice is neither science nor engineering—as we'll see soon—is "Why not? Why neglect technical investigation in favor of making spectacular but misleading demos?"

Part of the answer is "that's what you get paid for." As I suggested in "Create a negative public image for AI," a PR strategy has motivated spending tens of billions of dollars to wow the public, not to advance understanding. Figuring out what's going on inside backprop networks is hard work that mostly no one wants to pay for—especially not if it is likely to reveal unexpected risks and limitations.

Another part of the answer is that backpropaganda mythology says trained networks are inherently incomprehensible. Therefore, there is no point trying to understand them with science or with engineering analysis.

The inevitability of neural networks is the second myth. A natural question in response to "backprop is an engineering fiasco" is "so why does anyone use it, then?" The obvious answer is "because it can do cool stuff nothing else can." That is true today, but it's not the whole story.

Another piece is that people figure that since brains produce natural intelligence, artificial brains are the way to produce artificial intelligence.

Everyone working in the field knows "neural networks" are almost perfectly dissimilar to biological ones, but the language persists. "Yes, of course, everyone knows that, so it's harmless." No, it's not. And it's not just that it reliably confuses people outside the field, to the benefit of insiders.

It also confuses technical people, even when they know why it's misleading. It produces a pervasive, tacit sense of the inevitability of backpropagation as *the* essential and universal method for artificial intelligence. After all, we know brains can do intelligent thing X, so backprop must be able to do it too, so there's no point wasting time experimenting with alternatives.

Intellectual honesty and hygiene advise dropping the misuse of "neural" to describe backprop networks. This neuro-woo impedes safer AI.

THE MYTH OF INCOMPREHENSIBILITY OBSTRUCTS RATIONAL INVESTIGATION

Backpropaganda claims that trained networks are inherently incomprehensible. They work by intuition, not rationality. They are holistic, where the failed symbolic AI approach was reductionist. Their intelligence is spread throughout the network, which in recent systems contains hundreds of billions of adjustable values. They contain no explicit representations, so it's impossible to take them apart to find out what they're doing. You can only treat them as mysterious black boxes.

As we will see in the reverse engineering section, this is false. Backprop networks are composed—at least in part—of small, specific bits with identifiable functional roles. They don't work by holistic intuitive woo; they perform sensible computations, understandable in engineering terms.

However, the myth is convenient for both technical people and the decision makers who put systems into use.

For technologists, the supposed inscrutability frees you from an engineer's moral responsibility for understanding what your product is doing and how. That's hard work, and much less fun than building cool demos.

Inscrutability also frees technologists from understanding the messy, non-technical details of the particular real-world task you apply backprop to. It probably involves people, who are annoyingly unpredictable, so technologists don't like thinking about them. Backprop is supposedly a universal learning method, so it will figure out everything about the task for you, and you never need to know.

It's to the advantage of decision makers that technical people don't try to understand the application domain. If they looked into it, they might raise pesky safety concerns, or discover and publicize your dubious agenda.

For decision makers, inscrutability is an advantage if it makes it infeasible to hold anyone to account for bad consequences.[194] Authorities justify deployed, dubious AI systems by switching rapidly between rationalist and anti-rational descriptions, as rhetorically convenient. AI is unbelievably powerful cutting-edge high technology, and therefore you must use it. Simultaneously, it is inherently incomprehensible, so its errors cannot be explained, and therefore you have to accept them without question.

Alexander Campolo and Kate Crawford describe this strategy as "enchanted determinism." Deployed backprop networks are both "enchanted" (they work by magic) and determined (they are technologically inevitable). Therefore, whoever put one in place is absolved of responsibility for explaining or rectifying their harmful effects.

> We are not being confronted with a sublime form of superhuman intelligence, but a form of complex statistical modeling and prediction that has extraordinarily detailed information about patterns of life but lacks the social and historical context

---

[194]Joshua A. Kroll, "The fallacy of inscrutability," *Phil. Trans. R. Soc. A* 376:20180084, 2018.

that would inform such predictions responsibly—an *irrational rationalization.*[195]

Finally, the myth offers convenient rhetorical synergy with extreme risk and extreme benefit scenarios. If backprop networks can't be understood mechanistically, they must be treated as minds instead, which makes them Scary. If they can't be analyzed, there are no known limits to their capabilities. Then you can handwave their doing whatever implausible thing your narrative requires—whether it's destroying the planet or delivering utopia.

Backpropaganda's anti-rational rhetoric is an example of what I called *collective epistemic vice* in "Upgrade your cargo cult for the win":[196]

> Epistemic virtue and vice are not just *learned from* a community of practice, they *inhere in* it. The ways that community members interact, and the way the community comes to consensus as a body, are epistemically virtuous or depraved partly independent of the epistemic qualities of individuals. Just as moral preference falsification can lead a community of good people to do terrible things, epistemic preference falsification can lead a community of smart people to believe false or even absurd things.

NEURAL NETWORKS DON'T SOLVE PROBLEMS UNIFORMLY

Backpropaganda suggests neural networks can provide *general* artificial intelligence. They can do anything brains can do, so they're the right technology for every job. Implicitly, backprop is presented as effectively magic, able to solve any problem uniformly, without tedious task-specific engineering.

In fact, unaided it usually doesn't work at all. Seeming successes using bare backprop in the 1980s were mostly researchers fooling themselves.

---

[195]"Enchanted Determinism: Power without Responsibility in Artificial Intelligence," *Engaging Science, Technology, and Society*, Vol. 6, 08 Jan 2020. Emphasis added.

[196]At metarationality.com/upgrade-your-cargo-cult.

Recent successes come instead from combining backprop with task-specific mechanisms: convolutions for image processing, tree search for games, conventional amino acid sequence alignment methods for protein folding, and the complex transformer architecture for text generation. They also depend on extensive per-task fiddling with algorithmic variations that have no basis in theory.

The fundamental backprop algorithm is very simple. It's essentially the same as Newton's method for finding function maxima or minima via gradient descent. (You may remember that from an introductory calculus class; if not, it's not important for this discussion.[197]) Backprop's *gradient descent*[198] method attempts to minimize the difference, for each training data input, between the network's output and the correct output. That difference is the amount of *error* for the data item. Put a different way, backprop *optimizes* the network's fit to the data.

This basic algorithm makes mathematical sense, but it hardly ever works. Various kludgy add-ons address its typical failure modes. For example, minimizing error can lead to overfitting, so it's common to optimize some complex regularized function of the error instead. Such alterations to the algorithm are *ad hoc*, and not derived from theoretical principles. In most cases, their operation can be adjusted by turning "knobs" called *hyperparameters*. The effects of the hyperparameters are poorly understood.

Getting good results from backprop usually depends on setting several hyperparameters just right. There's no theoretical basis for that, and in practice "neural networks" get created by semi-random tweaking, or "intuition," rather than applying principled design methods. Often, no hand-chosen set works well, so researchers run a *hyperparameter search* to try out many combinations of values, hoping to find one that produces an adequate network. (Might this necessity for epicycles be a clue that the approach is overall wrong?)

It is widely acknowledged in the field that it is mysterious why backprop

---

[197] In a narrower, more technical usage, "backpropagation" refers only to one aspect of the algorithm: computation of error gradients layer-by-layer, caching intermediate results for efficiency. Commonly, though, "backpropagation" is used somewhat vaguely to refer to any gradient-based optimization method for "neural networks."

[198] You can blame the pun "Gradient Dissent" on @lumpenspace.

works at all, even with all this tweaking.[199] It's easy to understand why gradient descent works in the abstract. It's not easy to understand why overparameterized function approximation doesn't overfit. It's not easy to understand how enough error signal gets propagated back through a densely-connected non-linear deep network without getting smeared into meaninglessness. These are scientifically interesting questions. Investigation may lead to insights that could—ideally—help design a better replacement technology.

In current practice, however, getting backprop to work depends on hyperparameter search to tweak each epicyclic modification just right. Each modification to the algorithm has an understandable explanation abstractly, but none does the job individually, and it's not easy to understand why they work well enough in combination—when they do.

If it seems likely that the resulting system would have unpredictable properties and fragile performance… that is usually the case.

Historical accidents make backprop seem inevitable

Taking backprop as the sole, correct base technology for artificial intelligence may now seem an eternal certainty. However, while the neuro-mythology is ancient, it was considered a fringe ideology until a decade ago. Recent dramatic successes may have vindicated it. Alternatively, enormously increased funding, applied capriciously to a single dubious technology, may have forced progress in a less-than-optimal direction.

The inefficiency, inscrutability, and unreliability of backprop are serious shortcomings. I believe that the current dominance of this technology is a path-dependent accident of history.

In the software industry, it is common for technically inferior designs to overwhelm better alternatives if they gain early momentum. The initial lead may come from overfunding, successful marketing hype, incidental initial ease of use due to compatibility with other current technologies, or pure random accident. The dominance of backprop may depend on all these.

---

[199] See for instance Terrence Sejnowski's 2020 "The unreasonable effectiveness of deep learning in artificial intelligence," *PNAS*, December 1, 2020, vol. 117, no. 48, 30033–30038.

Specifically—looking ahead—backprop's early success depended on advances in consumer video graphics boards, and perhaps just some random luck. Then Mooglebook poured unprecedented amounts of money into backprop research, and used their enormous PR resources to hype results, sometimes inaccurately.

Minds vs. brains

From its beginnings in the late 1950s, AI research has been split between opposing factions: those based in theories about minds, and those based in theories about brains. Despite whole disciplines devoted to understanding minds and brains, the available theories of both are inadequate and probably fundamentally mistaken. This was a main reason AI made slow progress: turning our slight understanding of either minds or brains into software did not work.

According to the 1950s mainstream theory of minds, their essence is reasoning about knowledge. "Reasoning" was taken to mean logical deduction.[200] The research program that attempted to capture reasoning in software came to be known as "symbolic AI." That approach conclusively failed in the late 1980s. I was partly responsible for that conclusion, and the subsequent "AI winter" that lasted until about 2012.[201]

The reasons for symbolic AI's failure are not primarily technical, but follow from first principles. They are permanently fatal, I think.[202] In criticizing "neural networks," I am not advocating a symbolic alternative.

Perhaps translating some *better* understanding of minds into software might work. However, what little effort has been expended in that direction has not borne fruit to date.

The other main approach to artificial intelligence, from the beginning, has been to emulate brains. Those are mistakenly thought to produce natural

---

[200] As it became clear that was wrong, theorists in the 1970s tried to invent something similar to logic, yet somehow different. This "cognitive science" research program retained most of the central mistaken assumptions of logicism, and consequently failed.

[201] Sorry about that! I explain, sort of, in the "Artificial intelligence" section of "I seem to be a fiction" (metarationality.com/ken-wilber-boomeritis-artificial-intelligence).

[202] Part One of *In the Cells of the Eggplant* explains these reasons, in a broader context than just AI.

intelligence.[203]

"Neural networks" evolved from a 1940s theory of how biological neurons work.[204] The theory was wrong, and neuroscientists regard it as of only historical interest. It was influential in AI in the 1960s, but fell out of favor during the 1970s.

Neural networks were resurrected in the mid-80s as an alternative to symbolic AI, whose failure was then coming into focus. Surely there must be *some* way to create artificial intelligence! Neural networks were newly appealing as the exact opposite of symbolic AI. At minimum, they appeared to avoid its main defects: combinatorial explosions, inability to cope with nebulosity, and the need to hand-code knowledge.

When symbolic AI hit the wall, a hype train positioned neural networks as its designated successor. Advocates' enthusiasm for the neuro-mythology, opposed by mainstream researchers who understood why it was false, resembled a holy war in the mid-to-late '80s. The conflict depended on a false dichotomy, according to which *one* of the two approaches must be correct—whereas subsequent history suggests neither was.

By the early 1990s, backprop fizzled. Some seeming technical progress in the '80s, in applying it to small problems, turned out to be researchers fooling themselves. The rest turned out not to scale up to larger problems.

Anyway, most of the excitement had not been due to technical results, but to the revival of the notion that "neural networks" work like brains—and therefore *must* be the route to artificial intelligence.

Perhaps translating some *better* understanding of brains into software might work. However, what little effort has been expended in that direction has not borne fruit to date.

Backprop research wilted to the ground, and laid dormant under the snow of the AI winter for the next two decades. A few stubborn believers kept the roots alive, though.

---

[203] People, societies, and cultures produce intelligence, not brains. Brains are *involved*, as are (for example) stories. A brain would not be sufficient to produce intelligence, if one could somehow be disentangled from the person, society, and culture.

[204] Specifically, Donald Hebb's 1949 theory of learning built on a 1943 model of neurons due to Warren McCulloch and Walter Pitts, implemented in 1958 as the "Perceptron" by Frank Rosenblatt.

Forcing a brick airplane to fly

A funny but true adage of aeronautical engineering is that, by applying enough power, you can make a brick fly. Aerodynamic design makes an airplane safe and efficient, but it may limit top speed and it slows development. Alternatively, you can bolt an enormous engine onto an aerodynamically inferior body. This is common in fighter jets. The space shuttle took it to the max: a 184-foot, billion-dollar, use-once disposable engine, attached to a stubby airplane that was literally covered in bricks. Two of its 135 flights failed, killing everyone onboard both times.

During the AI winter, machine learning continued as an independent field devoted to statistical optimization methods. Neural networks were considered an eccentric subdiscipline, producing generally inferior results.

Mainstream machine learning research sought to overcome long-standing obstacles: overfitting, local minima, high computational cost, and a requirement for enormously more data than people need to learn the same things. Progress came from adopting unprincipled algorithmic hacks that often gave better performance on one or more of these dimensions, without theoretical justification.

Neural networks leapt out of obscurity in 2012, as winners—by large margins—of the ImageNet classification benchmark competition.[205]

What had changed—and what hadn't?

The new image classifiers benefited from two sorts of advances. First, they were much less "neural" even than 1980s systems. Those were emulations of 1940s biological models that had already long been known false, but at least they were faithful to the theory. The 2010s systems inherited, from the previous couple decades of machine learning practice, a willingness to incorporate atheoretical add-ons that empirically improve performance. In the case of the decreasingly-neural networks, those included devices such as max-pooling, batch normalization, and dropout. Those addressed problems such as overfitting and local minima, without reference to biological analogies.

---

[205] Most histories cite AlexNet's 2012 victory as the turning point. This seems accurate in terms of tech industry awareness. However, the similar DanNet also won by a large margin in 2011. This led to a bitter precedence battle between the senior members of the two research teams.

Second, the new neural networks ran on GPUs (Graphics Processing Units): add-on boards for home computers, designed to generate video game graphics. Inexpensive 2010 GPUs could do arithmetic faster than the million-dollar supercomputers of a few years earlier. They had also only recently been made suitable for general-purpose computing, not just graphics. Neural networks' enormous arithmetical cost had been a main drawback relative to other machine learning methods. GPUs made them competitive.

What *hadn't* changed was backprop's deceptive cunning. Once again it had fooled researchers by exploiting spurious correlations in the benchmark. The ImageNet results didn't mean what they seemed to, and success had little to do with neural networks. I discuss this in detail in the upcoming "Classifying images" section.

The dramatic ImageNet results drew the attention of the giant tech companies, including a bidding war to hire and fund the same senior neural network researchers who had led the 1980s movement.[206] Since then, they have put more funding into backprop than have gone into all other AI technologies combined throughout history.[207]

They've put enormous engine power into—what? Perhaps a brick airplane. Progress in artificial intelligence may be due to Mooglebook's unprecedented financial backing, and the consequent enormous efforts of a host of brilliant, highly motivated researchers, using unimaginably vast quantities of supercomputer time—rather than any intrinsic merit of backpropagation.

We can't know, but I'd guess we'd be in a better position if that funding, brilliance, and computation had gone into something else. Or, still better, into a variety of research approaches, to see which would yield the best combination of capability, efficiency, and safety. In any case, putting all the eggs

---

[206] Cade Metz, "The Secret Auction That Set Off the Race for AI Supremacy," *Wired*, Mar 16, 2021.

[207] I'm reasonably sure of this, but I haven't been able to find good numbers. From sketchy sources, it appears that total global AI research funding averaged well under a billion dollars per year before 2012; it now runs at many billions per year. Sevilla *et al.*'s analysis of the amount of computation used in machine learning runs provides relevant evidence: it has grown much faster than Moore's Law starting from 2012, and continuing to accelerate. "Compute trends across three eras of deep learning," *arXiv*:2202.05924, 2022.

in this one basket seems unwise.[208]

To be fair, no other AI approach had made much progress in decades; why throw good money after bad? On the other hand, no other approach had had much effort devoted to it during the AI winter, so the lack of progress may not have indicated much.

Still, it seems that the recent dominance of "neural networks" in the marketplace of ideas is due to backpropaganda as well as technical success. The major AI labs are headed by veterans of the 1980s neural-vs.-symbolic battles. They remain determined to prove that "neural" networks are the route to human-like AI *because* they are brain-like—even though they aren't.[209] As in the 1980s, they define themselves in defiance of symbolic AI, and are still stomping on that dead horse.

But did the "neural" approach win? Or did *ad hoc* algorithms with zero biological relevance successfully exploit supercomputers?

Dropping the neuro-mythology, the lesson of the past decade is that spending tens of billions of dollars on advanced software development can get you exciting results that have no basis in theory, that you don't understand, and that are unreliable and unsafe.

---

[208] Klinger *et al.*'s "A narrowing of AI research?" (*arXiv*:2009.10385v4, 11 Jan 2022) discusses this problem, plausible policy responses, and a framework for funders to broaden bets.

[209] To be fair, they also emphasize that current methods are insufficiently similar to brains, and advocate more biologically accurate models. Younger researchers mostly don't care about that. Since 2012, funding has pulled a huge number of new entrants into the field, most of whom know little about its history, and are motivated just to win benchmark competitions by whatever means.

Do AI as science and engineering instead

We've seen that current AI practice leads to technologies that are expensive, difficult to apply in real-world situations, and inherently unsafe. Neglected scientific and engineering investigations can bring better understanding of the risks of current AI technology, and can lead to safer technologies.

AI is unavoidably hybrid as an intellectual discipline. It incorporates aspects of six others: science, engineering, mathematics, philosophy, design, and spectacle. Each of these contributes valuable ways of understanding, and their synergies power AI insights. Different schools of thought within AI research have emphasized some disciplines and deemphasized others, which contributes to the schools' different strengths and weaknesses.

The current backprop-based research mainstream overemphasizes spectacle (the creation of impressive demo systems) and mathematics (optimization methods, misleadingly termed "learning"). It neglects science (understanding how and why the networks work) and engineering (building reliable, efficient solutions to specific problems). Naturally, this has led to powerful optimization methods which can yield spectacular results, but which we don't understand and which aren't reliable or efficient when applied to specific problems.

To address these problems, I suggest getting much more skeptical about spectacles; deemphasizing the math; and doing AI research as science and engineering instead.

Better understanding:

- May reveal that there is less to seemingly-spectacular results than meets the eye, thereby deflating hype (and consequently funding and deployment)

169

- May enable adding safety features to technologies similar to those we have now
- May lead to a full replacement of backprop and GPTs with quite different, safer technologies.

This chapter of *Gradient Dissent* draws on my 2018 essay "How should we evaluate progress in AI?"[210] That covers some of the same themes in greater depth; so you might like to read it if the discussion here is intriguing.

RUN-TIME TASK-RELEVANT ALGORITHMIC UNDERSTANDING

The type of scientific and engineering understanding most relevant to AI safety is run-time, task-relevant, *and* algorithmic. *That can lead to more reliable, safer systems. Unfortunately, gaining such understanding has been neglected in AI research, so currently we have little.*

It's common to explain that current AI systems are "neural networks," consisting of arithmetical "units" that are trained with "machine learning." This explanation is true as far as it goes, but it applies uniformly to extremely different AI systems, so it can't give much insight into what specific ones can or can't do, or why.

We need a different kind of explanation: one that can tell us how and when a system is likely to fail, and what to do about it

Run time is the operation of an AI system when deployed; it is what users see, and what can affect the world.[211] It contrasts with *training time*, which is the construction of the system using backprop. In current practice, these are entirely disjoint; a network is trained once, frozen, and does not change once put into use. Training time behavior is important for the people creating a system, but irrelevant for everyone else.

---

[210] At betterwithout.ai/artificial-intelligence-progress.

[211] Run time is also referred to with other terms, such as "inference time" and "feedforward computation." Usage doesn't seem to have standardized yet. There's a good analogy to compilation time vs. run time in conventional software, though.

We could distinguish three levels of analysis for any computational system.[212] The *black box* level describes what a system does, without explaining why or how. It considers only the input-output behavior. The *algorithmic* level explains why and how, abstractly. A full algorithmic analysis specifies the transformations that lead from each input to each output. The *mechanistic* level explains the specific machinery that accomplishes the algorithm.

One run-time black box explanation of a chatbot is "a program that accepts human-language inputs and produces often-appropriate human-language outputs." One run-time algorithmic explanation is that it alternates matrix multiplications with nonlinearly increasing function applications. One run-time mechanistic explanation is that the matrices are distributed to GPU memory and the multiplications are performed in parallel. These explanations are necessary for people building AI systems, but irrelevant for understanding them from a user or societal perspective.

They are nevertheless commonly given to the interested public, although they are quite useless. They give no insight into what the system is likely to do, right or wrong. They don't explain why the outputs are "often appropriate"; what sorts of inputs are likely to produce outputs that aren't appropriate; and what those outputs are likely to be instead.

It's also common to explain chatbots as "predicting the next word," which is true, but useless. Lacking the "why," it completely fails to explain what the chatbot actually does (which is *not*—from the user's point of view—predicting the next word). Lacking the "how," it says nothing about chatbots' capabilities and limits.

We need, instead, *task-relevant* run-time algorithmic understanding. That means understanding in terms relevant to wanted and unwanted behavior in the situation of use. It means insight into what a system can or can't do, and why. That can suggest both useful applications and risks.

Unfortunately, we don't have much task-relevant run-time algorithmic understanding, because little effort has been made to gain it.

- Far more research effort has gone into understanding training time than run time. This is an accident of history: current AI research

[212]This idea is originally due to the pioneering computational neuroscientist David Marr in 1976, and remains influential in cognitive science. I'm using different terms for the three levels than he did, but they're conceptually similar or identical.

culture descends from the machine learning field. Overemphasis on the the mathematics of optimization—which is what "training" means—encourages black-box thinking. It leads to neglect of the domain-specific reasons AI systems work.

- Research on task-relevant run time behavior has also mainly been at the black box level. Most is either haphazard observation of individually interesting outputs, or quantitative performance benchmarking—in both cases without attempting to answer "how" questions.

Run-time task-relevant algorithmic investigations are uncommon in AI research. The field rewards system performance, not understanding. It may take a huge amount of work to figure out what algorithms a network uses, because those emerge from training on a particular dataset, and weren't engineered in.

This is not an adequate excuse, in my opinion. Lack of attention to task-relevant run-time algorithms leads to AI systems that don't work well, because no one understands them. Then they can make inscrutable mistakes that may cause serious harms.

With task-relevant run-time algorithmic understanding, we should be able to:

- Find causes of good outputs, which may lead to new ways of enhancing them.

- Find causes of mistaken or unwanted outputs, which may lead to new ways of preventing them.

- Evaluate the likelihood of dangerous outputs in novel environments. We can do better than the current practice of feeding in lots of poorly-characterized input data and measuring how frequently we get bad outputs. This could help risk/benefit analysis before deployment.

- Predict what specifically what bad behavior is likely to occur under specifically which circumstances.

- Find better ways of improving systems than current practice. That is limited to "alter the optimization criterion" and "increase the pressure to conform to it." Those are at best limited, and arguably fundamentally flawed and unsafe.

- Find better technologies for accomplishing the sorts of tasks for which backprop is currently the leading contender.

We can get this kind of understanding with science; with reverse engineering; and with synergies between the two.

Science, in this case, proceeds by formulating task-relevant algorithmic hypotheses and devising and running experimental tests for them. We create hypotheses via analysis of the task dynamics, knowledge of general backprop behavior, understanding of human psychology and neuroscience, and informal observations of existing systems. I discuss an example in "Classifying images," later in this chapter.

Due to the complexity and inherent randomness of backprop networks, testing algorithmic hypotheses through examining input/output behavior may often be infeasible. Analyzing them at the mechanistic level first may yield algorithmic level insights. Sufficient mechanistic understanding—an explanation of how specific parts of the system contribute to its overall functioning—can reveal algorithms directly.

DO AI AS SCIENCE INSTEAD

Few AI experiments constitute meaningful tests of hypotheses. As a branch of machine learning research, AI science has concentrated on black box investigation of training time phenomena. The best of this work is has been scientifically excellent. However, the hypotheses tested are mainly irrelevant to user and societal concerns.

An nice example, with important practical applications, is the discovery of scaling laws for training text generators. These provide formulae relating training cost, network size, the quantity of training data, and predictive accuracy. They answer the question "if we plan to spend a specific number of millions of dollars on training, what are the best network size and training dataset size, and what predictive accuracy can we expect?" These laws have been replicated by multiple labs, and have significantly increased their efficiency.

I expect that these simple arithmetical laws can hold because bulk text is uniform in its statistical properties. That is, if you pull ten gigabytes of text from the web at random, it's going to look very similar to the next ten— even though particular text genres may have very different statistical properties. Training on academic chemistry journal articles won't let you predict the next word of social media chat, or vice versa, but if you slurp enough text at random, you'll get plenty of both.

What the scaling laws *don't* tell you is what a trained network can actually do—"capabilities" in the field's jargon. "Predictive accuracy" here is just the probability of predicting the next word of a previously unseen text. It doesn't tell you the probability that a chatbot's answers will be accurate or plausible but false, relevant or nonsensical, helpful or offensive. Empirically, predictive accuracy relates to task-relevant capabilities only loosely. Qualitatively new capabilities often emerge rather suddenly during training, even as predictive accuracy improves smoothly.

Scientific and mathematical analysis of optimization algorithms ignores the specific task the network is optimized for, and ignores the operation of the resulting network at run time. Those are what matter for practical applications and for safety. Real-world tasks are usually not amenable to mathematical analysis, due to their open-ended complexity. Overemphasis on mathematics has reinforced the field's "black box" approach.

AI research mainly aims at creating impressive demos, such as game-playing programs and chatbots, rather than scientific understanding. As I explained in "How should we evaluate progress in AI?",[213] such demos often do not show what they seem to—whether through carelessness in exposition, honest researcher confusion, or deliberate deception.

OpenAI's ChatGPT was explicitly released initially as a demo ("a low-key research preview"). The public was so excited by it—unexpectedly for OpenAI—that they turned it into a product. It's still mostly not clear what that product is good for, much less how it works.

---

[213]At metarationality.com/artificial-intelligence-progress.

Benchmark performance rarely reflects reality

Competitions to get the best score on "benchmarks" drive the creation of advanced AI systems. This motivates *ad hoc* kludgery rather than analysis and principled design.

Capabilities are the practical aim for AI research. Text generator capabilities are typically assessed using *benchmarks*—collections of quiz questions. A random subset of the problems are used as training data; then the network is tested against the remainder. For many benchmarks, it's considered exciting to get the error rate down below 50%.

Research often proceeds by comparative benchmarking: does algorithm A or B do better on the benchmark? This looks sort of like science, but it is *not science*. It is not, because the benchmarks are not meaningful means for evaluation, and because determining that algorithm A does 3% better on the benchmark than algorithm B tells us nothing about how or why.

Benchmarking incentivizes rapid, blind construction of systems by increased brute force, and by random tweaking to see what marginally decreases wrong outputs. Minimal effort goes into understanding what the networks do and how, and why they make the errors they do.

It's considered perfectly normal and acceptable to build and deploy systems that you don't understand and which give bad outputs much of the time. "We can keep decreasing the error rate" isn't an adequate justification if errors are costly, harmful, or potentially disastrous.

Benchmarks are also not objectively correct measures of performance. Most are rather haphazard collections of quiz problems assembled unsystematically and with minimal thought.

- Often the people employed to construct benchmark problems have no relevant expertise. Many benchmarks are crowd-sourced on platforms such as Mechanical Turk, and are full of both errors and spurious correlations.

- Many other benchmarks are constructed mechanically, by inserting random values in fill-the-blanks templates. It is not surprising that a statistical method can, in effect, recover simple templates from the pattern of examples, without "understanding" anything.

It's common for systems that get high scores on benchmarks to do dramatically worse when applied to seemingly similar tasks in practice.[214] One common reason is that the benchmark examples are dissimilar to real-world ones in unexpected ways.

Another is that half-baked benchmark construction often creates easily-exploited spurious correlations in the training data. This bedevils "reasoning" benchmarks in particular.[215]

Adversarial research versus confounding spectacles

Forceful debunking may be necessary to persuade AI researchers to do the necessary science instead of aiming for spectacular but misleading demos. That will require new incentives and institutions for adversarial research.

Trying to show you can get a system to do something cool—especially when it's *anything* cool, you don't much care what—is neither science nor engineering. That's the dominant mode in current AI research practice, though. This drives competition on benchmarks, and publicizing individual exciting outputs—texts and images—without bothering to investigate what produced them.

It is natural and legitimate to want to amaze people. You are excited about your research program, and you want to share that. Your research is probably also driven by particular beliefs, and it's natural to want to persuade people of them. A spectacular demonstration can change beliefs, and whole

---

[214] This is notably true of text generators; see Kiela *et al.*, "Dynabench: Rethinking Benchmarking in NLP" (*Proceedings of the 2021 Conference of the North American Chapter of the Association for Computational Linguistics*, pp. 4110–4124, June 6–11, 2021) for examples, explanations, and proposed remedies.

[215] There have been many studies demonstrating this; for example, Gururangan *et al.*, "Annotation Artifacts in Natural Language Inference Data" (*arXiv*:1803.02324v2, 6 Apr 2018); Timothy Niven and Hung-Yu Kao, "Probing Neural Network Comprehension of Natural Language Arguments" (*ACL Anthology* P19-1459, 2019); Patel *et al.*, "Are NLP Models really able to Solve Simple Math Word Problems?" (*arXiv*:2103.07191v2, 2021); McCoy *et al.*, "Right for the Wrong Reasons: Diagnosing Syntactic Heuristics in Natural Language Inference" (*Proceedings of the 57th Annual Meeting of the Association for Computational Linguistics*, 3428–3448, 2019); Dasgupta et al, "Language models show human-like content effects on reasoning" (*arXiv*:2207.07051v3, 2023). I don't know of any studies in which a text generator was found to "reason" reliably on a test that definitively eliminated the ability to cheat.

ways of thinking, in minutes—far faster than any technical exposition or logical argument.

The danger is in giving the impression that a program can do more than it does in reality; or that what it does is more interesting than it really is; or that it works according to your speculative explanation, which is exciting but wrong. The claims made in even the best current AI research are often misleading. Results (even when accurately reported) typically do not show what they seem to show. If the public learns a true fact, that the program does X in a particular, dramatic case, it's natural to assume it can do X in most seemingly-similar cases. But that may not be true. There is, almost always, less to spectacular AI "successes" than meets the eye. This deception, usually unintended, takes in researchers as well as outsiders, and contributes to AI's perennial hype cycle.

Zachary C. Lipton and Jacob Steinhardt attribute this to:

> "(i) failure to distinguish between explanation and speculation; (ii) failure to identify the sources of empirical gains, e.g., emphasizing unnecessary modifications to neural architectures when gains actually stem from hyper-parameter tuning; (iii) mathiness: the use of mathematics that obfuscates or impresses rather than clarifies…; and (iv) misuse of language, e.g., by choosing terms of art with colloquial connotations or by overloading established technical terms."[216]

The first two of these could be summarized as failure to perform control experiments: that is, to consider and test alternative possible explanations. A common bad practice, for instance, is to assume that a network has "learned" what you wanted it to if it gets a "good" score on a supposedly relevant benchmark. An alternative explanation, that it has gamed the benchmark by finding some statistical regularity other than the one you wanted, is more often true. That gets tested too rarely.

---

[216]Zachary C. Lipton and Jacob Steinhardt, "Troubling Trends in Machine Learning Scholarship" (*arXiv*:1807.03341, 2018). Also see Hullman *et al.*, "The worst of both worlds: A comparative analysis of errors in learning from data in psychology and machine learning" (*arXiv*:2203.06498, 2022) for a similar, detailed analysis.

Figuring out how and where and why backprop systems work will require shifting research incentives from spectacle to understanding. A conventional approach would try to shift academic peer review toward more careful application of proper scientific norms. This wouldn't work: because the most-hyped research is done in industrial labs, and because the field's *de facto* standards for peer review are so abysmal that reform, even if possible, would take much too long.

I suggest incentivizing *adversarial AI research* that would perform missing control experiments, with the expectation they will show that many hyped results do not mean what they seem to.[217] It would address questions like:

- Did it work for the reason the authors thought it did?
- If not, why did it work?
- Under what circumstances will it work, or not?
- What does it do when it *doesn't* work?
- What other methods might have worked better?
- Did they report all the things they tried that didn't work? No, they did not. For example, they ran thousands of hyperparameter combinations; how and why did most fail? We could probably learn from that, but mostly we don't because it's rarely attempted.

Fame and funding should flow to researchers who answer these questions. This demands unusual funders, and unusual researchers.

Funders want to see "progress." This research program aims at *negative* progress in spectacle generation. Ideally, its results should be disappointing to the public. It should progress scientific understanding instead. That is more valuable in the long run, but it may take unusual fortitude for funders to accept the tradeoff.

---

[217]I did several such experiments around 1990. Mostly I didn't bother to publish them, because I guessed (correctly) that backprop would fizzle when other people realized the then-hyped results were mostly researchers fooling themselves. I did write up one in "Input Generalization in Delayed Reinforcement Learning: An Algorithm and Performance Comparisons" (with Leslie Kaelbling; *Proceedings of the International Joint Conference on Artificial Intelligence*, 1991). We found that a success story for reinforcement learning with backprop worked slightly better when we replaced the backprop network with a linear perceptron, and we could explain why the perceptron worked in task-relevant terms.

Most researchers don't do control experiments, or enough of them, unless they are forced to. Control experiments are boring, a huge amount of work, and are likely to show that your result is less interesting than you hoped. There are many possible explanations for any result; ruling out all of them except the exciting one takes much more work than futzing around with a network to get it to produce some cool outputs. Control experiments seem like janitorial scutwork.

What could motivate researchers to do other people's janitorial scutwork, to clean up the mess? Some researchers *actually care about the truth*, and are naturally attracted to this sort of work. Watching hype overwhelm concern for truth also gets some of us angry, in a useful way. It's an unattractive but important fact that annoyance with other researchers' carelessness drives much of the best scientific work.

Competitiveness also motivates benchmark-chasing ("we beat the team from the Other Lab!"). I expect it's feasible to shift some of that emotional energy to "we showed that the Other Lab were fooling themselves and they were *wrong*, hah hah!"

This debunking must concentrate on the *best* work; 90% of research in all fields is of course crud, and not worth refuting. The aim should be to demonstrate ways even the best is misleading (it over-claims, overgeneralizes, fudges, cherry-picks, etc.). Some AI critics do this now, which is valuable, but their analyses are relatively shallow and abstract ("the system doesn't **really** understand language, because look, it gets these five examples wrong"). That's not their fault; detailed control experiments take a lot of work and computational resources.

The psychology replication movement would be a valuable model. Many of that field's long-held beliefs were due to researchers fooling themselves with inadequate controls, non-reporting of negative results, overgeneralizing narrow findings, refusing to make code and data available to other researchers to analyze, and other such epistemological failures.[218] This got some young researchers angry enough to force major incentive changes. Those make newer work far more credible.

---

[218] See "How should we evaluate progress in AI?" and "Troubling Trends in Machine Learning Scholarship" for discussion of many other questionable research practices and specific epistemological errors.

Researchers chase funding and prestige. Explicit calls for proposals for adversarial work could motivate with funding. Prizes could motivate with prestige.

Academia is a more natural environment for debunking than industry. However, given the magnitude of the task, academic AI labs may not be a good structure for the scale required. An independent "adversarial AI lab" might concentrate the necessary resources. A Focused Research Organization might provide the right structure for the task.[219]

DO AI AS ENGINEERING INSTEAD

Current AI practice is not engineering, even when it aims for practical applications, because it is not based on scientific understanding. Enforcing engineering norms on the field could lead to considerably safer systems.

Work in AI is often described as "engineering." It's highly technical, it certainly isn't science, and it's not just mathematics, so it must be engineering by process of elimination? It's most likely to be called "engineering" when it aims toward practical application, with the idea that engineering consists of solving practical problems with technology. That definition includes too much, though; most things you do with a computer (or even in the kitchen) solve practical problems with technology, and definitely aren't engineering.

The American Engineers' Council for Professional Development definition:

> The creative application of *scientific principles* to design or develop structures, machines, apparatus, or manufacturing processes, or works utilizing them singly or in combination; or to construct or operate the same with *full cognizance* of their design; or to *forecast their behavior under specific operating conditions*; all as respects an intended function, economics of operation and *safety to life and property*.

---

[219]A Focused Research Organization is a special-purpose institution created to solve a single scientific or technological challenge that is too large for an academic lab, too small for a national Big Science project, and that lacks the short-term path to profit required of private startups. See astera.org/fros/.

I have added *emphasis* on features of engineering mainly absent from current AI practice.

Considerable genuine engineering has gone into getting known optimization algorithms to run efficiently on available hardware, and into designing new hardware that will run known algorithms faster. However, the algorithms themselves are not derived from engineering; they are not based on scientific principles, they are not rationally designed, we have very limited ability to forecast their behavior, and safety is at best an afterthought.

Fiddling with hyperparameters to get a better benchmark score—the main mode of AI system development—is not engineering. Much effort also goes into finding inputs ("prompts") that that *somehow* yield "good" outputs. That is also not engineering.

This judgement is not an arbitrary or values-neutral matter of definition. It's a matter of norms; of the ethic and ethos of engineering. The chief engineer for a bridge construction project should be the first to drive across it. A sane engineer does not trust a bridge that "only" failed three percent of the time in a simplistic simulation.

The black box tinkering methodology *has* created amazing things. This practice of intuitive exploration of mechanism variations might be worthy of meta-level investigation as a *new way of knowing* that is neither science nor engineering.[220] This could be a fascinating project in epistemological theory.

It would not, however, excuse the field from addressing serious safety questions before its products are deployed. There's currently no known way to do that apart from conventional science and engineering.

Task-relevant mechanistic understanding with reverse engineering

Current practice mainly treats backprop networks as inscrutable black boxes. Opening them up to examine their operation often reveals that they work in straightforward ways. That should make them amenable to reengineering for greater safety and better performance.

Current AI research retains the machine learning field's emphasis on "learning," meaning error minimization algorithms, and neglects investigation of what trained networks do and how. For this reason, there may be an

[220]Michael Nielsen's "The role of 'explanation' in AI" (*Sporadica*, 09-30-2022) makes this case. Subbarao Kambhampati's "Changing the Nature of AI Research" (*Communications of the ACM*, Volume 65, Issue 9, pp 8–9) is a somewhat skeptical discussion of the approach.

unconscious slip from recognizing that the "learning" phase is mysterious to assuming that the run-time computation is too. It's almost taboo to look inside the black box to find out how the network operates at run time. That often turns out to be less mysterious than the emergence of capabilities during training.

We can break open backprop networks to find out how they do what they do, in task-relevant mechanistic terms. This is analogous to reverse engineering, except that backprop networks aren't engineered. Molecular biology is another analog: understanding how metabolic pathways and genetic regulatory networks work by probing and teasing apart the many specific molecular interactions that make them up.

Investigations typically find that small pieces of backprop networks compute the sorts of things you'd expect them to given the task requirements.[221] For example, specific circuits within image classifiers detect edges, which has been known for decades as critical in both mammalian and conventional machine vision systems.[222] Feed-forward modules in GPTs act as key-value stores, with individual units representing specific facts.[223]

Altering one of those little bits causes the network to change the corresponding specific functionality, while retaining the rest. For example, a series of studies have found that specific facts, such as that the Eiffel Tower is in Paris, can be located in GPTs, and then the few relevant parameters can be directly modified so the model "believes" the Tower is in Rome.[224]

Such knowledge, accumulated, dispels the aura of magic. It suggests that the network as a whole can be made comprehensible; and perhaps made less impressive, once understood in task-relevant mechanistic terms.

This level of understanding explains, for example, why vintage-2022 image generators could produce photorealistic pictures of horses, but put the

---

[221] Much of the best work in this area has been done by Chris Olah and his collaborators. For an overview as of 2020, see their "Thread: Circuits" (distill.pub/2020/circuits/).

[222] Olah *et al.*, "An Overview of Early Vision in InceptionV1," distill.pub/2020/circuits/early-vision/.

[223] Dai *et al.*, "Knowledge Neurons in Pretrained Transformers," *arXiv*:2104.08696v2, 2022.

[224] For a summary of one such study, plus a useful literature review, see Meng *et al.*, in "Locating and Editing Factual Associations in GPT," rome.baulab.info. As of late 2022, the state of the art is Meng *et al.*, "Mass-Editing Memory in a Transformer," *arXiv*:2210.07229v2.

wrong the number of legs on them about 20% of the time.[225] That doesn't matter for safety, but analogous errors do. If leg count were critical, forcing the error rate down just with more stringent training would be an inherently unsafe approach. Neel Nanda's "Longlist of Theories of Impact for Interpretability"[226] discusses safety benefits of task-relevant mechanistic understanding.[227]

Reverse engineering a backprop network is not so different from reverse engineering legacy code. Analogs of familiar methods work:

- *Instrument the code*: Add apparatus that lets you trace the network's computation at run time. For example, Meng et al. developed a technique for locating the pathways through a GPT network that correspond to particular facts.[228] Several researchers have developed "lens" methods that reveal how each layer in a transformer refines the prediction of the next word.[229]

- *Construct small artificial test cases*: Nanda *et al.*'s full reverse engineering and mechanistic explanation of a small network optimized for modular arithmetic is a fascinating, beautiful example.[230] It probably gives significant insight into the operation of large models (although this remains to be demonstrated).

---

[225] As of September 2022, according to François Chollet, a prominent researcher in the area, at twitter.com/fchollet/status/1573879858203340800. Getting body part counts right (fingers are especially difficult) has been a main focus of improvement in image generator development since then.

[226] *LessWrong*, 11th Mar 2022.

[227] This is often termed "interpretability" in machine learning research, but that term is overloaded and confusing; see Zachary C. Lipton's "The Mythos of Model Interpretability," *arXiv*:1606.03490, 2016.

[228] Meng *et al.*, "Locating and Editing Factual Associations in GPT," *arXiv*:2202.05262v5, 2022.

[229] For example, Belrose et al., "Eliciting Latent Predictions from Transformers with the Tuned Lens," *arXiv*:2303.08112, March 2023.

[230] "Progress measures for grokking via mechanistic interpretability," *arXiv*:2301.05217, 12 Jan 2023.

- *Minimize naturally-occurring test cases*: Instead of building bigger GPTs to improve benchmark performance, we should see how small we can make them while maintaining performance. Smaller networks are likely to be easier to understand. (The upcoming "Better text generation" section covers this.)

- *Automate diagnostic methods*: Determining the function of bits of a network is mainly still a painstaking manual process, requiring significant human intuition. However, as methods for that are validated and systematized, they can be automated; some early work of this sort has been demonstrated.[231]

- *Alter the system to make it easier to understand, without significantly changing functionality*: For example, Elhage *et al.* demonstrated that making a small, theoretically-motivated change to the activation function decreases polysemy of units in a GPT while retaining performance.[232] Filan *et al.* describe regularization and initialization methods for increasing the modularity of networks in a graph cut framework.[233]

Engineering safer AI

Ideally, software should be proven correct. That is unusual in current software engineering practice. However, responsible software development projects require, at minimum, unit testing (checking that each of the parts works in isolation), integration testing (the system works as a whole), and code review (every part of the program gets examined for possible errors by someone other than its author).

We should require analogous practices when backprop nets are deployed in situations in which errors matter. That would be very expensive currently, but objecting to that is like complaining that safety engineering for cars is expensive. If you want to manufacture automobiles, you have to pay that cost.

---

[231] For example, in Conmy et al., *"Towards Automated Circuit Discovery for Mechanistic Interpretability,"* arXiv*:2304.14997, 28 Apr 2023.

[232] Elhage *et al.*, "Softmax Linear Units," transformer-circuits.pub/2022/solu/index.html.

[233] Filan *et al.*, "Clusterability in Neural Networks," *arXiv*:2103.03386v, 2021.

Making this a requirement would incentivize developing better testing and debugging tools. I expect those are possible, given recent progress, and given how little effort has been put into developing them so far.

Typically, when you understand the function of a piece of a network, you find that it computes that only probabilistically and approximately. In some cases, researchers can replace those bits with deterministic, engineered, exact equivalents. For example, Cammarata *et al.* successfully replaced backprop-derived curve-detection units in an image classifier with manually engineered ones.[234] Such re-engineering may increase reliability without affecting performance.

Ideally, the entire network could be replaced with a deterministic, fully understood, engineered alternative. This should be an AI safety engineering goal.

Engineered systems can't be guaranteed absolutely safe. Even if we understand exactly what a device does, its interaction with unpredictable situations will be inherently unpredictable. You can't engineer a perfectly safe car, because of black ice, landslides, and drunk drivers. Cars are statistically safer than horses, however; engineered solutions can be more predictable than those that emerge from an optimization process, whether backprop or evolution.

CLASSIFYING IMAGES: MASSIVE PARALLELISM AND SURFACE FEATURES

Analysis of image classifiers demonstrates that it is possible to understand backprop networks at the task-relevant run-time algorithmic level. In these systems, at least, networks gain their power from deploying massive parallelism to check for the presence of a vast number of simple, shallow patterns.

In this section, I'll explain some of what is known about how backprop-trained image classifiers work—and how they don't. GPTs are currently less well understood than image classifiers; my guess is that similar explanations

---

[234]"Curve circuits," distill.pub/2020/circuits/curve-circuits/.

What is wrong with this picture?

apply. If so, we should be less impressed with them, and perhaps less frightened.

I'm writing this section as a personal narrative, partly because the way I came to understand image classifiers may make me overconfident in my guesses about GPTs. Knowing how I came to my tentative conclusions will let you discount them accordingly.

Shortly after finishing a PhD in AI in 1990, I ignored the field until 2014, because nothing seemed to be happening. In 2014, I came across the dramatic AlexNet image classification results from two years earlier, and was shocked. AlexNet wasn't *scary*; just unexpected, and initially inexplicable.

I felt I absolutely had to understand what was going on. Back around 1990, I had done some work in machine vision and some with backprop networks, and I understood the states of those fields as of then. It didn't seem like backprop should be able to do as well as the AlexNet ImageNet benchmark results showed.

The traditional approach to object recognition in machine vision research was to start from a 2D image of (say) a teapot, and build a reconstruction of the 3D shape that would look like that when viewed from a particular angle. Then you could rotate the 3D reconstruction to match against a database of 3D models of different object categories. I couldn't see any realistic way a backprop network could learn to do that. Humans have special purpose mental rotation hardware, which didn't seem like it would emerge naturally from backprop training.

So this was an irritating anomaly, especially because my experience had been that backprop networks are very good at fooling backprop researchers, and very bad at solving whatever problem they were set. I definitely didn't want the backprop advocates to finally be right about something. On the other hand, there didn't seem to be any obvious way for the networks to cheat on the ImageNet task.

So I read a bunch of papers, which didn't help me understand what was going on. But I also thought about the nature of the problem itself.

One of the last bits of AI work I did was laying the groundwork for a pancake-making robot. I chose that task because my view was that an essential limitation of AI was its inability to cope with *nebulosity*—the fuzzy, gloppy, formless quality of reality. Pancake batter is gloppy, and pancakes cooked on a griddle have no definite shape. That meant that traditional robotics and machine vision methods, which were designed for teapots and other rigid manufactured objects with fixed shapes, wouldn't work.

I set myself as a subtask the machine vision problem of determining when it is time to flip a pancake—which is when bubbles have emerged fairly uniformly on the top, and the batter starts to look less glossy. I figured I'd video cooking many pancakes and see if I could write a detector for the moment of flippability.

So what mattered here was texture, rather than shape. Machine vision research had done very little with texture, although it seemed to me that it might be important in many visual tasks. There was a theory of "textons," fundamental units of texture, which no one had implemented. To do that, you'd need to run a slew of different convolutions over the image. Unfortunately, the computers of the era ran at about one megaflops, so computing even a single convolution took ages. After messing around with that a bit, I concluded that I wasn't going to get anywhere any time soon.

AlexNet, running on two 2012 GPUs, was engineered specifically to compute lots of convolutions fast, so it seemed plausible that texture detection was part of how AlexNet worked. What else was it doing? Well, detecting small 2D features is also something that sort of network could do. But those don't add up to object recognition. Do they?

Hmm, one other trick would be to exploit spurious correlations between the environments (background) in which an object typically appears and the object type. Exploiting spurious correlations was known to be a common way for backprop networks to cheat.

And also, snapshots on the internet (the basis for the training dataset) usually photograph objects from typical angles, so approximate 2D shape matching might work, without 3D reconstruction and rotation.

So it should be easy to test this. Could AlexNet be fooled by showing it images that humans would instantly identify unambiguously?

The example I thought of was a toilet seat (an unusual, fixed, easily identified shape), covered in zebra skin fabric (a texture that would not be associated with toilet seats in the training data), photographed at an unusual angle (so 2D shape matching wouldn't work), in an outdoor natural landscape (where you might find zebras but not usually toilet seats). I started writing a piece about this, and nearly rushed out to actually make and photograph one to test. Then I reined in my disobedient brain, and told it firmly that someone else would presumably figure this out—if, in fact, the explanation was right.[235]

Over the next few years, a series of fascinating experiments showed that it *was* right.[236] In fact, my thought experiment was gross overkill. Image clas-

---

[235]I've been told that unspecified others figured this out earlier, but they didn't write it up at the time.   My work on this was in December 2014 and January 2015. My earliest public mention, as far as I can find, was on 13 February 2016 (twitter.com/Meaningness/status/698688687341572096). I'm mentioning dates not to establish academic priority, but to suggest that my predictions about AI may be credible.

[236]For a non-technical summary, see Jordana Cepelewicz's "Where we see shapes, AI sees textures," *Quanta Magazine*, July 1, 2019.

sifiers get fooled with any *one* of the tricks I had in mind.

- Artem Khurshudov reported a similar experiment, based on the same analysis: all of several AlexNet-like systems classified a picture of a leopard-print sofa as a leopard.[237]

- Samuel Dodge and Lina Karam found that blurring or adding random noise to images radically degraded classifier performance, while leaving images recognizable (with a bit of difficulty) for humans. As a possible explanation, they suggested that "the network may be looking for specific textures."[238]

- Moosavi-Dezfooli *et al.* found that adding a tiny amount of a single, fixed pattern of noise, virtually undetectable by humans, caused misclassification of *most* images. The pattern was high frequency and edge- and curve-dense (messing with texture) and brightly colored (messing with color clues).[239]

- Engstrom *et al.* found that rotating and translating images degraded classification too.[240]

- Carter *et al.* tested the hypothesis that classifiers cheat by exploiting correlations between object types and the backgrounds they are typically photographed against. They found that classifiers did well when shown only narrow strips of the image, around its borders, including zero pixels from the object itself.[241]

---

[237]"Suddenly, a leopard print sofa appears" (May 2015). Some systems did get his original image right, but all classified the sofa as a leopard if he rotated it 90 degrees. I only discovered his discussion several years later.

[238]"Understanding How Image Quality Affects Deep Neural Networks," *arXiv*:1604.04004, April 2016. It had been known for a couple years that classifiers could be fooled by adding noise crafted to be "adversarial" against an individual image (Goodfellow *et al.*, "Explaining and Harnessing Adversarial Examples," *arXiv*:1412.6572, December 2014). As far as I have found, this was not previously attributed to breaking texture clues, and also Dodge and Karam's work was the first demonstration that random noise was effective.

[239]"Universal adversarial perturbations," *arXiv*:1610.08401v1, October 2016.

[240]"Exploring the Landscape of Spatial Robustness," *arXiv*:1712.02779, December 2017.

[241]"Overinterpretation reveals image classification model pathologies," *NeurIPS* 2021.

- To test the texture-only hypothesis, Wieland Brendel and Matthias Bethge randomly scrambled the global structure of images, leaving texture intact, and found it did not badly degrade classification performance.[242] Apparently local information is more discriminating even than I had imagined; large-scale 2D shape matching doesn't add much value. This is consistent with image generators such as DALL-E producing photorealistic pictures of horses that have five legs, as in the example from François Chollet at the beginning of this section. "A [neural network] model is excellent at reproducing local visual likeness, yet it has no understanding of the parts & their organization."[243]

- Olah *et al.* performed a series of circuit-level analyses of the guts of classifier networks, and identified specific circuits computing texture elements, local feature detectors (for dog noses, for instance), and 2D shapes (for cars, for instance). Car detectors look for car windows above car wheels, and don't work on upside-down cars (which humans have no difficulty with).[244]

In sum, it seems that, at the task-relevant algorithmic level, an image classifier mainly consists of an extremely large number of mainly small-scale, highly specific 2D feature detectors. It computes all those in parallel, and classification relies on a small number firing that together predict a particular image category.[245]

---

[242]"Approximating CNNs with Bag-of-Local-Features Models Works Surprisingly Well on ImageNet," *ICLR* 2019. A similar and earlier but perhaps less definitive test was Baker *et al.*'s "Deep convolutional networks do not classify based on global object shape," *PLOS Computational Biology*, 2018.

[243]At   twitter.com/fchollet/status/1573836241875120128   and   twitter.com/fchollet/status/1573843774803161090.

[244]For a summary of this research, "Zoom In: An Introduction to Circuits," distill.pub/2020/circuits/zoom-in/, 2020.

[245]In more recent work, researchers have found ways of training networks to use shape information more and texture less, which does improve performance. Geirhos *et al.*, "ImageNet-Trained CNNs Are Biased Towards Texture; Increasing Shape Bias Improves Accuracy and Robustness," *ICLR* 2019; Dehghani *et al.*, "Scaling Vision Transformers to 22 Billion Parameters," *arXiv*:2302.05442, 2023.

It's plausible that one could engineer a non-"neural," more efficient and better understood system specifically for this purpose, by implementing the same algorithm in conventional software.

I'd like to generalize four hypotheses from the image classification example. Whether these apply in any other specific domain is an empirical question. At minimum, they seem worth pursuing as simple explanations of first resort, by Occam's Razor.

- Backprop isn't magic, and networks usually work in straightforward ways that make sense in terms of the task they're applied to.

- What we learned from AlexNet and its successors was not "backprop is incredibly powerful"; it was "texture clues are much more discriminating than previous theories of vision anticipated." This is a fascinating fact *about images*, not about backprop. Convolution computation was built in by the researchers, not discovered by backprop. Plausibly, other backprop successes similarly rest on a combination of specialized researcher-given architecture and unexpectedly simple, brute-force solutions to apparently complex problems.

- It's usually possible to figure out what a network is doing: from first principles in the case of my guess, and then by experimental tests, and then by detailed circuit analysis.

- Typically, networks gain their power from deploying massive parallelism to check for the presence of a vast number of simple, shallow patterns. I believe current text generators work this way too.

I think this must *also* be much of the way brains work, because neurons are so slow. Biological circuits are extremely depth-limited. We too must rely on breadth for our own, limited smarts instead. This was a motivating constraint in my PhD work. It is a *valid* similarity between "neural" networks and the brain—whereas artificial "neurons" and backprop aren't.[246]

---

[246] For an insightful exploration of this theoretical perspective, see Hasson *et al.*, "Direct Fit to Nature: An Evolutionary Perspective on Biological and Artificial Neural Networks," *Neuron*, Volume 105, Issue 3, 5 February 2020, Pages 416-434.

BETTER TEXT GENERATION WITH SCIENCE AND ENGINEERING

Current text generators, such as ChatGPT, are highly unreliable, difficult to use effectively, unable to do many things we might want them to, and extremely expensive to develop and run. These defects are inherent in their underlying technology. Quite different methods could plausibly remedy all these defects. Would that be good, or bad?

Good or bad? A conundrum

My interest in AI, briefly rekindled in 2014 by the ImageNet results I discussed in the previous chapter, fell mainly dormant again until mid-2022. Then I learned of newly-discovered "chain-of-thought" behavior in text generators, in which they appeared to engage in common sense reasoning. Common sense reasoning has been the holy grail of AI research from the beginning.[247] It's plausibly the way AI could transcend the limitations of interpolation (discussed in "Beyond interpolation: reasoning," earlier).

Automated common sense has been stubbornly resistant to progress, and this seemed a potential breakthrough—perhaps with both exciting and scary implications.

Rapid technical progress in text generation alarmed many other people, too. Will a few more years development at that rate produce Scary superintelligence? We don't know, and we should try to find out. The work I did mid-2022 made me think it's unlikely, and subsequent developments have tended to reinforce that, but this conclusion remains tentative.

Prudence therefore advises recognizing that Scary AI *might* arrive soon, and acting accordingly. We should try to find out by doing science and engineering on the systems we already have, not by rushing ahead full tilt building more powerful ones to see whether or not they cause an apocalypse.

Reasoning about how current text generators work synergized both with work I had done in computational linguistics thirty years earlier and with in-

---

[247]John McCarthy's 1958 paper "Programs with common sense" (*Proceedings of the Teddington Conference on the Mechanization of Thought Processes*, 756–91) was an immensely influential founding document of the field.

sights from my analysis of image classifiers. Together these may have profound implications for fundamental linguistics and cognitive science, which I find extremely exciting! They also suggest several ways it may be feasible to build systems with functionality similar to that of current text generators, but based on different technology that would make them reliable, easier to use, more powerful, and more efficient.

Would that be good? The behavior of the mechanisms I have in mind would be much more predictable than current systems, and therefore much less likely to become Scary for unknown reasons. That's good!

On the other hand, if they are more powerful, reliable, and inexpensive, they are much more likely to be used—and abused. They might have larger unpredictable effects on the world than the current program of building ever-larger, more expensive versions of ChatGPT using the same "predict next word" paradigm. That's probably bad!

Since better text generation technologies might have either good or bad effects relative to the current path, I have been torn, ever since I started this project, about how much to say about them.

I suspect the project of scaling up GPTs may be approaching its limits. Existing text generators get trained on pretty much all the text worth training on, and may do nearly as good a job of processing it as is possible within the current technological paradigm. ChatGPT, despite predictions both of enormous short-term economic benefits and apocalyptic disemployment of most office workers, has had no broadly visible effects in its first year of existence. It may not be feasible to increase the usefulness of such systems much further, in which case the tens of billions of dollars going into attempts may be wasted.

Then the current wave of AI enthusiasm may recede, as previous ones have. On balance, I think that would probably be good, because so far we have no clear path to a good future with powerful general-purpose AI, and plenty of plausible disaster scenarios. Among current AI approaches, text generation seems the most worrying, due to its seeming reasoning ability. If it's the most dangerous current technology, and may be approaching its limit, we can be less concerned for now about Scary AI. So this suggests that my explaining ways to make *better* ChatGPT-like systems would be bad.

As I am still extremely unsure about this, I will describe only the least innovative and seemingly safest of the several possibilities I envision. Regretfully, I am omitting discussion of less obvious, more powerful, more dangerous possible future language technologies.

Not to keep you in suspense, the approach I *will* describe is to separate language ability from knowledge. A dramatically smaller GPT can provide fully fluent text generation, drawing content from a well-defined textual database, rather than mixing up facts with its language ability. That would eliminate the current biggest defect of GPTs: "making stuff up" or "hallucinations."[248] Separating language and content makes outputs faithful to the text database. Shrinking the GPT by several orders of magnitude would also make it much easier to analyze, understand, and validate.

Text prediction: the wrong tool for the job

Current mainstream text generators are all based on the GPT (generative pre-trained transformer) architecture. That works by taking as input some text (a "prompt") and predicting a statistically plausible continuation of it.

Plausible text continuation has little, if any, inherent usefulness.

This paradigm was not originally *intended* to be useful. Useful text generators were an unexpected, accidental byproduct of computational linguistics research. The primary goal was to understand syntax: the grammar of human languages. The technical approach built a statistical model of a pile of human-written text. A system that could output grammatically correct English, without someone having to encode all the grammatical rules, was the aim.

No one imagined that the grammatical but meaningless gibberish it output ("colorless green ideas sleep furiously") would be of any use. That would be the whole next research project, in which the grammatical model would get connected to a knowledge representation and reasoning system. The reasoning system would produce meanings, and the linguistic system would translate those into English, and thereby serve as its output channel.

It turned out that if you train on *huge* quantities of human-written text, the outputs are not only grammatical, they often seem meaningful. Initially, as in GPT-2, only for a sentence or two; but then scaling up from "huge" to

[248]The term "hallucination" is misleading; in all other contexts, the word refers to perceptual phenomena, which this is not. "Bullshit," in the quasi-technical sense of Harry Frankfurt (*On Bullshit*, 2009), would be more accurate. When a speaker or writer doesn't care—or often even *know*—whether their seeming claims are true, they are generating "bullshit" in this sense. That is precisely what current AI text generators do.

"unimaginably gigantic," as in GPT-3, they'd generally sound sensible for a paragraph or two. Such systems seemed to be learning semantics (meanings) as well as syntax (grammar).

And, researchers discovered that careful crafting of prompts could produce outputs that were not only internally meaningful, but relevant and useful. In the simplest case, something like "What is the capital of France?" causes the output "Paris is the capital of France," because in the training data that's the most common next sentence. A large enough GPT is able to answer questions like this even when the question and answer are not literally paired in the training data, because it finds patterns in the forms of questions and corresponding answers.

This discovery was completely unexpected,[249] and is now the primary positive use for text generators. (Probably the *economically* dominant use is in boilerplate generation, for spam and near-spam, whose overall value is negative.)

Text generators are still usually referred to by researchers as "language models," although modeling *language* hasn't been their purpose in many years. Later in this chapter, I suggest that it *should* be: a GPT should model *language*, not the contents of a random terabyte of blather scraped from the web.

Text generators' near-omniscience is the basis of much current excitement, fear, financial investment, marketing hype, and research effort. This is largely misconceived and misdirected, however. At best, a text generator "knows" only what was in its training dataset, and in the best case it would just report that accurately, in full or in summary as requested.

Unfortunately, GPTs can't and don't do that. They are only trained to produce statistically plausible continuations of their inputs. Those include confident explanations of plausible-sounding falsehoods that are *not* in the texts they were trained on.

In a meaningful sense, they don't "know" anything at all. They are text genre imitation engines, not knowledge bases. As I wrote earlier,

> It is not that text generators "make stuff up when they don't know the right answer"; they don't *ever* know. If you ask one whether quokkas make good pets, it may write a convincing

---

[249] Petroni *et al.*, "Language Models as Knowledge Bases?", *ACL Anthology* D19-1250, 2019.

article explaining that they are popular domestic companions because they are super friendly and easy to care for. Ask again immediately, and it may write another article explaining that they are an endangered species, illegal to keep as pets, impossible to housebreak, and bite when they feel threated. Exactly the same process produces both: they are mash-ups of miscellaneous internet articles about "does animal X make a good pet," with some quokka factoids thrown in.

This is not a reasonable basis for most of the things people want text generators to do. They are the wrong tool for the job. It's amazing how well they work considering that, but the overall approach is fundamentally and unfixably flawed.

Nevertheless, proponents are trying to make GPTs seem inevitable as the way forward for AI in general, because they want to sell something *now*.

As retrieval mechanisms for textual knowledge, GPTs compete with web search. Or, they compete in principle, at least! In practice, as of 2023, they are mostly complementary, with the strengths of each partially compensating for the defects of the other. The approach I suggest in the next section should combine the strengths of both.

- The greatest defect of GPTs is "hallucination," generating authoritative-sounding text full of artificially-generated falsehoods. The advantage of web search is that it may lead you to an actually authoritative and accurate human-written text. GPTs are configured to go out of their way to avoid giving you human-written text, even when they have memorized it verbatim, probably for copyright reasons.

- Web search provides lists of whole documents, parts of which may ideally be relevant to your query. You still need to read or search through each document to find the bit or bits that might answer your question. GPTs provide a single concise output that ideally is fully relevant and provides a full answer. On the other hand, it may be unhelpful vaguely-relevant-sounding nonsense, or actively misleading and false.

- Web search may also lead you to authoritative-sounding web pages that are full of falsehoods and meaningless blather, written by GPTs, or by "content farms" that employ poorly-paid workers who have no relevant knowledge, or by random internet crazies. This has gotten much worse in the past couple years (partly because of automatically generated web spam). The average quality of GPT answers is probably better than the *average* quality of web search results.

- Web search can mostly only lead you to texts that are available in full on the web. Much of the highest-quality information is in books and periodicals that are not. GPTs appear to have *de facto* access to those. It's widely believed that they are trained on entire research libraries containing tens of millions of books—or the equivalent, via the Sci-Hub and Z-library "pirate" document databases. The big AI labs are extremely cagey about their training data, plausibly because it is of dubious legality under copyright law. Text generators are an end-run around copyright: by rephrasing content, they obfuscate their sources. Unfortunately, in so doing, they may also distort them into misinformation.

Separating linguistic ability from knowledge

I suggest that separating these could produce a reliable human-language interface to a database of human-language text, eliminating ChatGPT's hallucinations; providing concise, relevant, detailed answers (unlike web search); and giving access to the knowledge in books and periodicals not available on the web while avoiding copyright violation.

I'll first sketch the way this might work, and then describe some recent research that suggests it is feasible, along with some historical context. I won't go into technical details, nor answer objections that the approach wouldn't work for one reason or another. In this case, that is not for safety reasons, it's because I don't have any unusual insights into the technical considerations. This is a minimally innovative proposal, and anyone working in the field will see the same possibilities and obstacles I do.

For several years, text generation researchers pursued the "scaling hypothesis" that larger networks yield better performance, possibly without bound.[250] Extensive empirical evidence seemed to bear this out: almost always, bigger networks did better on benchmarks. Eventually, a lottaflops and as much as a hundred million dollars were spent training single networks on the order of a trillion parameters, and they did better than ones with only tens of billions. Increasing evidence suggests that by late 2022 this had run its course, however.

In retrospect, it seems likely that the main reason scaling up GPTs improved benchmark performance was that in effect they store the text they were trained on—somewhat compressed and distorted—in form of network parameters.[251] Many standard benchmarks test mainly knowledge, so storing more of it (in near-textual form) gives better test performance.

We tend to mistake omniscience for intelligence, because we cannot imagine what it would be like to have instant mental access to the most relevant knowledge in a major research library containing tens of millions of books.

However, backprop networks are an extraordinarily expensive and unreliable way to store text. Probably a quite small network can capture full linguistic fluency, if it doesn't need to waste parameters on "knowing" stuff as well. Then it can rely on the actual original text for its "knowledge," instead.

Starting in 2020, several teams recognized that a GPT often behaves *as though* it is retrieving text, and basing its output on that, although it doesn't in fact have access to any. So they augmented GPTs with a large text database, available at run time, and a semantic-match retrieval engine.[252] And this works dramatically better!

For example, in August 2022, the retrieval-augmented Atlas GPT set new state-of-the-art accuracy records on various "language understanding" and "knowledge intensive" tasks with an 11 billion parameter network, out-

---

[250] Gwern   Branwen,   "The   Scaling   Hypothesis,"   gwern.net/scaling-hypothesis,   2020.   This   is   related   to   Rich   Sutton's   "Bitter   Lesson," www.incompleteideas.net/IncIdeas/BitterLesson.html, 2019.

[251] This is not the only reason, but the others aren't relevant here.

[252] Guu *et al.*'s "Retrieval augmented language model pre-training" (REALM) was among the pioneers; *Proceedings of the 37th International Conference on Machine Learning*, PMLR 119, 2020. Borgeaud *et al.*'s "Improving language models by retrieving from trillions of tokens" (RETRO) scaled the method up and made many improvements; *arXiv*:2112.04426v3, 7 Feb 2022.

performing PaLM, the previously most powerful GPT, which had 540 billion parameters.[253] It's fifty times more efficient on that metric.

This suggests that the increasing performance of larger networks was due in large part to assimilating increasing quantities of text. Retrieval-augmented GPTs are a success story for an agenda I described earlier: replacing parts of backprop networks with engineered alternatives, based on algorithmic-level understanding, making them more efficient, interpretable, and reliable.

Taking this approach to the limit, there seems no good reason to allow "knowledge" in network. We should want to get rid of that! Ideally, we should want a retrieval-*only* system, not a retrieval-*augmented* one. A fluent but ignorant text generator could reliably summarize responsive content from its text database, eliminating "hallucination." It could link the passages it drew on, so you could assess their quality and relevance.[254]

One reason text generators are still mainly unsafe for commercial use is that their output could be based on anything found in a terabyte of who-knows-what. A customer service chatbot should reliably base answers solely on a company-specific database. That may be feasible with this architecture. Many companies are experimenting with retrieval augmentation for this reason; but unless the generator is fully ignorant, its outputs are based unpredictably on the text it was originally trained on, retrieved text, and a mixture of the two.

An advantage of retrieval-augmented systems is that the text database can be updated at near-zero cost. Outputs based on retrieval immediately reflect that change. In contrast, correcting mistaken, unwanted, or out-of-date "knowledge" in a plain GPT requires at minimum "fine tuning" (partial retraining, which is quite expensive), and potentially complete retraining (prohibitively expensive).

Retrieval augmentation's update capability is limited, though, because outputs are based only in part on retrieved text. In a retrieval-*only* system, you'd have total, near-zero-cost control over what "knowledge" outputs derive from.

---

[253] Izacard *et al.*, "Few-shot Learning with Retrieval Augmented Language Models," *arXiv*:2208.03299v3, 2022.

[254] Chirag Shah and Emily M. Bender make an interesting case against this, though, in "Situating Search," *CHIIR '22*, March 2022, pp. 221–232.

Why isn't everyone already doing this?

So if this is such a good idea, why isn't everyone doing it? The retrieval-only ideal seems obvious. I proposed it in October 2022,[255] but no one else has mentioned the possibility, as far as I have seen, much less pursued it.[256] Even retrieval augmentation seems radically underused relative to its benefits, and I don't know why.

Maximizing reliance on retrieval may be a bad idea for some reason I'm missing. Or, I've thought of a couple of possible explanations for why it's not pursued. I'll describe a technical one and a public relations one.

The technical issue is run time compute cost. Because an ignorant language-only GPT would be much smaller than current typical ones, it would be much less costly both to train and to run. However, semantic retrieval from a terabyte text database has an additional computational cost. Sources I have read provide contradictory evidence for how this compares to GPT run time cost: some say it is much less, and others that it is much more.[257] How the cost scales with the size of the text database is also unclear.

This *might* be an insuperable obstacle. On the other hand, comparatively little effort has gone into optimizing it. Improved algorithms or faster implementations of existing ones might do the trick. If not, a different hardware architecture may be required. The fundamental operations for GPT run time and for retrieval are quite different. Neural network computation is dominated by low-precision multiplication, which current AI supercomputers optimize with specially designed hardware. Semantic retrieval uses an enormous inverted text index, which maps text "meanings," i.e. points in latent space, to corresponding text fragments. Computation cost is dominated by access to the RAM storing the index. Retrieval is highly parallelizable, so an optimal architecture might use a very large number of SIMD CPUs with high-bandwidth RAM buses.[258]

[255] twitter.com/Meaningness/status/1576195630891819008.

[256] An exception may be Lan *et al.*'s "Copy Is All You Need," *arXiv*:2307.06962, 13 Jul 2023.

[257] Mitchell A. Gordon's "RETRO Is Blazingly Fast" (on his personal web site, Jul 1, 2022) is an example of the first; Min *et al.*'s "Silo Language Models" (*arXiv*:2308.04430, 8 Aug 2023) is an example of the second.

[258] Ironically, perhaps, this was the architecture of the 1980s Connection Machine AI super-

Anyway, greater compute cost might be worth paying. It buys you safety and reliability that a straight GPT can't provide, even if it's more expensive than just blurting out whatever seems plausible.

Another reason major AI labs may not have pursued the retrieval-only approach is that it seems a step backward from their stated goal of creating artificial *general* intelligence. Using "instruction tuning,"[259] plus a gigantic, convoluted, secret "system prompt," a gigantic GPT can be coaxed into the appearance of performing many dissimilar tasks. That makes plausible "We're leaders on the path to omnipotent superintelligence!" This claim, rather than mundane utility, is the basis for the colossal financial investment into the big AI labs.

The retrieval-only paradigm is not necessarily applicable to all the things people try to make GPTs do currently. It's plausible that versions of this approach could address some of the other tasks large GPTs are used for now, but probably not all. For example, a linguistically sophisticated but ignorant system might be able to provide a conversational "chat" interface to its text database, or to an API. It might not be able to write boilerplate without a detailed spec (a major current application for GPTs), or to provide the "creative" functions of story writing or brainstorming.

That seems *good*. "Tool AIs" that do specific things reliably are safer than superintelligent AGI, and more likely to provide net positive utility.

Retrieval-only systems could be dismissed as **just** better search engines. ("Google Search already does this! It uses semantic matching (sometimes) to retrieve from the web, and uses a GPT to summarize results (sometimes).") From my point of view, this technical unimpressiveness is *good*.

I expect most people would rather have simple software that does one thing reliably than a technically complex *spectacular demo* which does a vast but unspecifiable collection of things, and often produces outputs that look correct and aren't.

Worries that GPTs may soon become secretly spookily smart, or possibly are already Scary, would not apply to an ignorant summarization engine. It's

computer, which was originally intended to process semantic networks. W. Daniel Hillis, *The Connection Machine*, 1986.

[259] Ouyang *et al.*, "Training language models to follow instructions with human feedback," *arXiv*:2203.02155, 4 Mar 2022.

inherently limited in what it can do. Further, ignorance would make GPTs dramatically smaller. Those will be easier to analyze, understand, and validate.

How to make an ignorant GPT

It's probably impossible to make a useful GPT is that entirely ignorant, and also probably impossible to make one that is entirely reliable and hallucination-free. The methods I sketch here may go a long way, but a GPT is still a GPT, and GPTs are still *The Wrong Thing*.

The boundary between world knowledge and linguistic ability is somewhat nebulous. Retrieval-*only* is an ideal, but not possible even in principle. Semantic disambiguation often depends on factual knowledge, some of which must therefore be included. Therefore, there's no precise criterion for what should be excluded, but most cases are clear enough. "Who pitched for the winning team in the 1909 World Series" does not belong in a GPT.

I believe entirely different approaches could deterministically produce language to order (instead of semi-randomly predicting likely continuations). This was always the goal in AI research until a few years ago, when GPTs proved unexpectedly capable. I see no reason to think it's impossible, although the methods attempted so far have not worked well. As mentioned earlier, I won't discuss this further, partly for safety reasons.

GPTs store vastly more world knowledge than linguistic knowledge, so just limiting network size is part of the recipe for ignorance. However, experience with training small networks (up to about seven billion parameters) on large text databases is that their language capability is poor. They are limited in what they can say, not just in how much they know.

During training on a large text dataset, a GPT doesn't "know" whether it's supposed to be memorizing text or inferring linguistic patterns, so it winds up doing some of each, mostly the first. To create an ignorant but linguistically fluent GPT, we'll need to bias it away from content learning and toward language learning.

Evidence that this may be feasible is provided by the TinyStories project.[260] Researchers trained tiny GPTs on a synthetic text database

---

[260] Ronen Eldan and Yuanzhi Li, "TinyStories: How Small Can Language Models Be and Still Speak Coherent English?", *arXiv*:2305.07759v2, April 2023.

consisting only of kindergarten-level stories, with restricted vocabulary and subject matter. The resulting systems produced fluent, coherent stories, several paragraphs long, with almost perfect grammar. They also demonstrated "reasoning" capabilities similar to those of large GPTs. These systems had around ten million parameters, three orders of magnitude fewer than "small" GPTs that are less linguistically capable, and five orders of magnitude smaller than current large ones. This is a proof of principle for the power of small GPTs when deliberately trained for competence rather than memorization. However, the TinyStories text database is restricted to a limited vocabulary and simple grammar.

Researchers followed up with a series of studies training small GPTs on databases of sophisticated, high quality text. Historically, because GPTs were intended as *language models*, they were trained on any old language, indiscriminately sourced from the internet. Because GPTs are extremely inefficient learners, enormous quantities of text was required. Unsurprisingly, they learned vast quantities of false facts and bad behavior from data such as political web forum disputes. It's becoming increasingly clear that text *quality* trumps quantity—another reason the scaling hypothesis seems increasingly shaky.

In "Textbooks Are All You Need" and other studies,[261] researchers showed that small GPTs trained on high-quality text perform as well on "language understanding" and "common sense reasoning" benchmarks as mainstream ones an order of magnitude larger. The data sets were a mixture of manually-curated high quality web text and synthetically generated text meant to cover "common sense knowledge."[262]

This suggests training a minimal-sized GPT on synthetic text that covers the full vocabulary and spectrum of linguistic constructions in a major research library, but with artificially minimal factual content. That might meet the simultaneous goals of language mastery and adequate ignorance. Con-

---

[261] Li *et al.*, "Textbooks Are All You Need II: phi-1.5 technical report," *arXiv*:2309.05463, 11 Sep 2023.

[262] These systems are straight GPTs, not retrieval-augmented, with about a billion parameters to store the knowledge. If the Atlas 1:50 ratio held up, a retrieval-augmented equivalent might have on the order of a hundred million parameters. In 2022 linguistic work (unpublished), I estimated the intrinsic complexity of language at roughly ten to a hundred million bytes on a quite different basis, consistent with this.

structing such texts would be a significant research project, but it's not obviously impossible, or even particularly difficult.

Alternatively, there may be ways to bias the training process itself toward finding linguistic patterns rather than storing content. It's also not obvious how to do that, but not obvious that it would be difficult or impossible.

Ignorance and copyright

Ignorant retrieval and summarization systems face roughly the same legal issues under copyright law as mainstream, knowledgeable GPTs. However, they may provide an opportunity for a win-win outcome not available to knowledgeable GPTs.

Large GPTs are trained mainly on copyrighted text and images. Numerous lawsuits by authors and publishers are underway, alleging that this use infringes copyright. There is no directly relevant legislation or case law as yet, and the overarching *fair use doctrine* is "murky and evolving." The outcome of these suits is, therefore, highly uncertain.[263] At one extreme, courts could rule that any use of copyrighted text in training constitutes infringement. At the opposite, they could rule that it constitutes fair use, even when GPTs output chunks of the copyrighted work verbatim (as they occasionally do). Probably they'd prefer some middle ground, whose shape is as yet undetermined.

AI companies' defense may depend primarily on the "transformativeness" aspect of copyright doctrine. They can argue that GPTs rarely reproduce copyrighted material verbatim (and they can take further technical measures to prevent them from doing so). Automated paraphrasing may constitute adequate transformativeness to avoid copyright infringement—or it may not. These considerations are much the same for an ignorant system, although its paraphrases may be closer to the source material on average.

A practical, rather than legal, defense for AI companies is that it's usually impossible to determine which texts contributed to a large GPT's output. A plaintiff claiming copyright infringement may have a hard time demonstrating that it occurred. ("Yes, we trained the GPT on your book, but you can't

---

[263] For an overview of the legal issues and how they interact with technical ones, see Henderson *et al.*, "Foundation Models and Fair Use," *arXiv*:2303.15715, 28 Mar 2023. I took the phrase "murky and evolving" from this paper.

show that in any specific instance the GPT relied on it to produce supposedly-infringing output. It may, for instance, have relied instead on some similar book, or on a third-party summary of yours, maybe in a book review.") This defense does not apply to retrieval-based generation: the exact sources are knowable.

However, that provides an avenue of practical defense for retrieval-based systems not available to current mainstream ones. They can provide users with links to the sources used to generate an output. Sometimes users will then purchase copies of the linked copyrighted works. This suggests a possibility for a win-win outcome.

There is an analogy here with Google Books, which searches over tens of millions of copyrighted works and displays "snippets" of them for free. In 2005, authors and publishers filed suits alleging infringement. Google spent years working with the plaintiffs to craft a financial deal to compensate them for revenue lost when users read free snippets instead of buying the whole book. After a decade of tentative settlements that the plaintiffs couldn't quite agree to, the court finally ruled in favor of Google: snippets are fair use.[264]

So the authors and publishers technically lost, but it seems they still came out ahead. Users do indeed purchase books based on snippets significantly often. Those serve, in effect, as free advertising.[265]

Here's the deal that's a win for users, AI companies, authors, and publishers:

- Retrieval-based systems can include any and all copyrighted works in their run time databases, and base outputs on them;

- As long as they don't output more than snippet-length chunks of the works, this constitutes fair use;

[264] This was Authors Guild v. Google.

[265] Abhishek Nagaraj and Imke Reimers, "Digitization and the Market for Physical Works: Evidence from the Google Books Project," *American Economic Journal: Economic Policy* vol. 15, no. 4, November 2023, pp. 428–58. "We study the impact of the Google Books digitization project on the market for physical books. We find that digitization significantly boosts the demand for physical versions and provide evidence for the discovery channel."

- *Or*, companies running such systems might be obligated to pay copyright holders under a compulsory licensing scheme, at a rate determined by negotiation, legislation, or a court;

- Such systems are obligated to disclose the sources used for any output, with purchase links when those are provided by the copyright holder.

A better future, without backprop

If we must have AI, we should replace "neural" methods with simpler, cheaper, and safer alternatives.

The biggest worry for most AI doom scenarios are AIs that are deceptive, incomprehensible, error-prone, and which behave differently and worse after they get loosed on the world.

That is precisely the kind of AI we've got.

This is bad, and needs fixing.

"Artificial intelligence" is a vague term for "software that does something it's surprising for software to be able to do." Current text and image generation systems fit that definition. However, calling them "neural" or "AI" puts them in a special category, in which it may seem ordinary software engineering considerations do not apply. I think that's a mistake.

Reframing them as "expensive, poorly designed, buggy software rushed prematurely to market" dispels the mystical aura.

The lesson of "Forcing a brick airplane to fly" was that spending tens of billions of dollars on an ill-considered software development project as a PR stunt can get you amazing functionality, at the price of reliability. I expect that if you spend tens of billions of dollars to develop similar capabilities while aiming for scientific understanding and engineering quality control, you can get that instead.

Software history is replete with inferior technologies achieving "lock-in" by accident or brute force. Such dominance typically lasts only a decade or two.

I find it probable that neural networks and GPTs will be superseded by better, quite different techniques, within a decade perhaps. I provide no proposal for what those might be. It's reasonable, then, to object to the whole

207

of *Gradient Dissent* with "there is no alternative." That is true; but it may be only because no serious attempt has been made to find any.

Some single method may be easier to apply, more reliable, and more understandable, as well as making more efficient use of both data and hardware. Alternatively, a uniform "learning" technology that can bypass the hard work necessary to understand and solve particular problems may remain a pipedream for the forseeable future.

Instead, adequate algorithmic understanding of particular task domains may lead to the replacement of neural networks with diverse better technologies. Those would include a statistical component, but might be primarily conventional software. In any case, they should result in systems that are much easier to understand and control. Such alternatives might be equivalently or more powerful; orders of magnitude more efficient; amenable to conventional engineering methods; and more reliable.

"AI" shades into "advanced computational systems," which may be quite different from any current technology. We cannot accurately anticipate what those may be capable of. They may have large beneficial or harmful effects.

It would be wise, in future, to pay greater attention to potential risks than we've done with backprop-based AI.

www.ingramcontent.com/pod-product-compliance
Lightning Source LLC
Chambersburg PA
CBHW070837300326
41935CB00038B/1052